SIXTH EDITION

GRAMMAR 3B IN CONTEXT

SANDRA N. ELBAUM

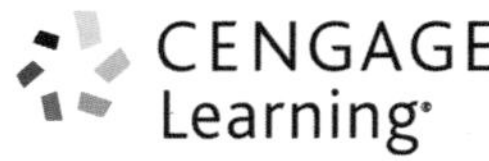

Australia • Brazil • Mexico • Singapore • United Kingdom • United States

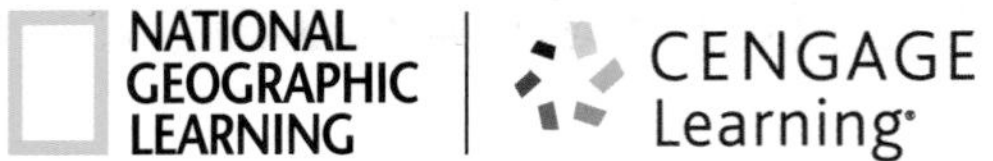

Grammar in Context 3B, Sixth Edition
Student Book
Sandra N. Elbaum

Publisher: Sherrise Roehr
Executive Editor: Laura Le Dréan
Development Editor: Claudi Mimó
Executive Marketing Manager: Ben Rivera
Senior Director, Production: Michael Burggren
Content Project Manager: Mark Rzeszutek
Manufacturing Planner: Mary Beth Hennebury
Interior Design: Brenda Carmichael
Compositor: SPi Global
Cover Design: Brenda Carmichael

ISBN 13: 978-1-305-07555-9

National Geographic Learning
20 Channel Center Street
Boston, Massachusetts 02210
USA

Cengage Learning is a leading provider of customized learning solutions with office locations around the globe, including Singapore, the United Kingdom, Australia, Mexico, Brazil, and Japan. Locate our local office at international.cengage.com/region

Cengage Learning products are represented in Canada by Nelson Education, Ltd.

Visit National Geographic Learning online at **ngl.cengage.com**
Visit our corporate website at **www.cengage.com**

Printed in the United States of America
Print Number: 01 Print Year: 2015

CONTENTS

GRAMMAR **Adverbial Clauses and Phrases**
Sentence Connectors (Conjunctive Adverbs)
***So/Such That* for Result**
CONTEXT **Coming to America**

GRAMMAR **Noun Clauses**
CONTEXT **Children**

GRAMMAR **Unreal Conditionals**
Wishes
CONTEXT **Science or Science Fiction?**

APPENDICES

GLOSSARY OF GRAMMATICAL TERMS

INDEX

ACKNOWLEDGMENTS

I am grateful to the team at National Geographic Learning/Cengage Learning for showing their faith in the *Grammar in Context* series by putting their best resources and talent into it. I would especially like to thank Laura Le Dréan for driving this series into an exciting, new direction. Her overall vision of this new edition has been a guiding light. I would also like to thank my development editor, Claudi Mimó, for managing the difficult day-to-day task of polishing and refining the manuscript toward its finished product. I would like to thank Dennis Hogan, Sherrise Roehr, and John McHugh for their ongoing support of *Grammar in Context* through its many editions.

I wish to acknowledge the immigrants, refugees, and international students I have known, both as a teacher and as a volunteer with refugee agencies. These people have increased my understanding of my own language and taught me to see life from another point of view. By sharing their observations, questions, and life stories, they have enriched my life enormously.

This new edition is dedicated to the millions of displaced people in the world. The United States is the new home of many refugees, who survived unspeakable hardships in Burundi, Rwanda, Iraq, Sudan, Burma, Bhutan, and other countries. Their resiliency in starting a new life and learning a new language is a tribute to the human spirit.

—Sandra N. Elbaum

Heinle would like to thank the following people for their contributions:

Dorothy S. Avondstondt, Miami Dade College—Wolfson Campus;

Pamela Ardizzone, Rhode Island College;

Patricia Bennett, Grossmont College;

Mariusz Bojarczuk, Bunker Hill Community College;

Rodney Borr, Glendale Community College;

Nancy Boyer, Golden West College;

Charles Brooks, Norwalk Community College;

Gabriela Cambiasso, Harold Washington College;

Julie Condon, St. Cloud State University;

Anne Damiecka, Lone Star College — CyFair;

Mohammed Debbagh, Virginia Commonwealth University;

Frank DeLeo, Broward College;

Jeffrey DiIuglio, Boston University Center for English Language and Orientation Programs;

Monique Dobbertin Cleveland, Los Angeles Pierce College;

Lindsey Donigan, Fullerton College;

Jennifer J. Evans, University of Washington;

Norm Evans, Brigham Young University—Hawaii;

David Gillham, Moraine Valley Community College;

Martin Guerra, Mountain View College;

Eric Herrera, Universidad Técnica Nacional;

Cora Higgins, Bunker Hill Community College;

Barbara Inerfeld, Rutgers University;

Barbara Jonckheere, California State University, Long Beach;

Gursharan Kandola, University of Houston;

Roni Lebrauer, Saddleback College;

Dr. Miriam Moore, Lord Fairfax Community College;

Karen Newbrun Einstein, Santa Rosa Junior College;

Stephanie Ngom, Boston University Center for English Language and Orientation Programs;

Charl Norloff, International English Center, University of Colorado Boulder;

Gabriella Nuttall, Sacramento City College;

Fernanda Ortiz, University of Arizona;

Dilcia Perez, Los Angeles City College;

Stephen Peridore, College of Southern Nevada;

Tiffany Probasco, Bunker Hill Community College;

Elizabeth Seabury, Bunker Hill Community College;

Natalia Schroeder, Long Beach City College;

Maria Spelleri, State College of Florida, Manatee-Sarasota;

Susan Stern, Irvine Valley College;

Vincent Tran, University of Houston;

Karen Vlaskamp, Northern Virginia Community College—Annandale;

Christie Ward, Intensive English Language Program, Central Connecticut State University;

Colin Ward, Lone Star College—North Harris;

Laurie A. Weinberg, J. Sargeant Reynolds Community College

A WORD FROM THE AUTHOR

My parents immigrated to the United States from Poland and learned English as a second language as adults. My sisters and I were born in the United States. My parents spoke Yiddish to us; we answered in English. In that process, my parents' English improved immeasurably. Such is the case with many immigrant parents whose children are fluent in English. They usually learn English much faster than others; they hear the language in natural ways, in the context of daily life.

Learning a language in context, whether it be from the home, from work, or from a textbook, cannot be overestimated. The challenge for me has been to find a variety of high-interest topics to engage the adult language learner. I was thrilled to work on this new edition of *Grammar in Context* for National Geographic Learning. In so doing, I have been able to combine exciting new readings with captivating photos to exemplify the grammar.

I have given more than 100 workshops at ESL programs and professional conferences around the United States, where I have gotten feedback from users of previous editions of *Grammar in Context*. Some teachers have expressed concern about trying to cover long grammar lessons within a limited time. While ESL is not taught in a uniform number of hours per week, I have heeded my audiences and streamlined the series so that the grammar and practice covered is more manageable. And in response to the needs of most ESL programs, I have expanded and enriched the writing component.

Whether you are a new user of *Grammar in Context* or have used this series before, I welcome you to this new edition.

Sandra N. Elbaum

For my loves
Gentille, Chimene, Joseph, and Joy

Welcome to **GRAMMAR IN CONTEXT,** Sixth Edition

Grammar in Context presents grammar in interesting contexts that are relevant to students' lives and then recycles the language and context throughout every activity. Learners gain knowledge and skills in both grammar structures and topic areas.

New To This Edition

NATIONAL GEOGRAPHIC PHOTOGRAPHS introduce lesson themes and draw learners into the context.

LESSON
7
Adjective Clauses, Descriptive Phrases
ONLINE INTERACTIONS
Patrick Meier analyzes social media and satellite imagery to help with relief efforts around the world.
The dream behind the Web is of a common information space in which we communicate by sharing information. Its universality is essential.
—Tim Berners-Lee

New To This Edition

EVERY LESSON OPENER includes a quote from an artist, scientist, author, or thinker that helps students connect to the theme.

NEW AND UPDATED READINGS, many with National Geographic content, introduce the target grammar in context and provide the springboard for practice.

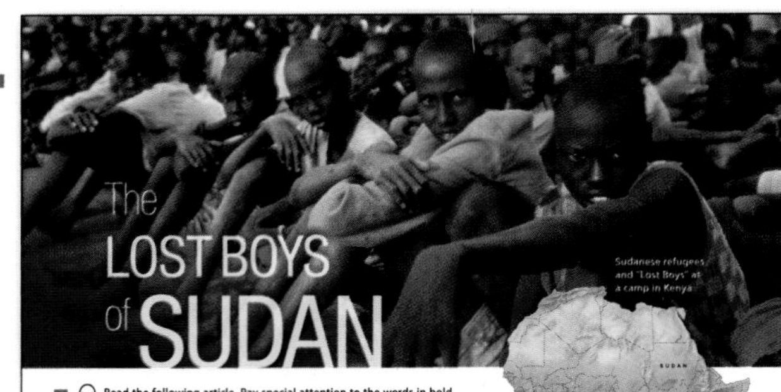

The
LOST BOYS
of SUDAN
Sudanese refugees and "Lost Boys" at a camp in Kenya
SUDAN
SOUTH SUDAN
ETHIOPIA
KENYA

NEW LISTENING EXERCISES reinforce the grammar through natural spoken English.

CD 2 TR 14 Read the following article. Pay special attention to the words in bold.

Besides immigrants, the United States takes in thousands of refugees a year. The Lost Boys of Sudan were children, living in southern Sudan in the late 1980s, when their long and difficult journey to the United States began. **While** these young boys were in the field taking care of their cattle,[3] their villages were attacked. These children, mostly boys between the ages of 4 and 12, ran for their lives. **For** three months, they walked hundreds of miles **until** they reached Ethiopia. They survived by eating leaves, roots, and wild fruit.

During that time, many died of starvation[4] and disease or were eaten by wild animals. Those who reached Ethiopia stayed in refugee camps **until** 1991, when a war started in Ethiopia and the camps were closed. They ran again, back to Sudan and then to Kenya, where they stayed in refugee camps **for** almost ten years. Of the approximately 27,000 boys who fled Sudan, only 11,000 survived.

During their time in the refugee camp, they got some schooling and learned basic English. In 1999, the United Nations and the U.S. government agreed to resettle 3,800 Lost Boys in the United States.

When they arrived in the United States, many challenges awaited them. They had to learn a completely new way of life. Many things were new for them: apartment living in a big city, strange foods, new technologies, and much more. **When** they saw an American supermarket for the first time, they were amazed by the amount of food. One boy was so surprised by the quantity of food in a supermarket that he asked if it was the palace of the king.

Agencies helped the Lost Boys with money for food and rent for a short time **until** they found jobs. **While** they were working, most of them enrolled in ESL classes. Now men, many have graduated from college and have started projects to help their villages back home. Peter Magai Bul, of Chicago, helped establish a school in his hometown. **While** he was studying for his college degree, Peter helped to raise funds for this school, which is currently educating over five hundred South Sudan students.

Although their future in the United States looks bright, **whenever** they think about their homeland, they are sad because so many of their family members and friends have died.

[3] *cattle:* cows, bulls, and oxen as a group
[4] *starvation:* the state of having no food, being extremely hungry

Connecting Ideas **257**

COMPREHENSION CHECK Based on the reading, tell if the statement is true (**T**) or false (**F**).

1. The Lost Boys were in a refugee camp in Ethiopia until they came to the U.S.
2. When their villages were attacked, the Lost Boys ran back home.
3. Some of the Lost Boys are helping their people in South Sudan.

9.3 Time Clauses and Phrases

NEW REDESIGNED GRAMMAR CHARTS offer straightforward explanations and provide contextualized clear examples of the structure.

Examples	Explanation
When their villages were attacked, the Lost Boys ran. Some young men will help their people back home **when** they finish college.	*When* means "at that time" or "immediately after that time." In a future sentence, we use the present in the time clause.
Whenever they think about their country, they are sad. **Whenever** they tell their story, Americans are amazed.	*Whenever* means "any time" or "every time."
They walked **until** they reached Ethiopia. They received money for a short time **until** they got jobs.	*Until* means "up to that time."
Peter has been a student **since** he came to the U.S. He has been working **(ever) since** he arrived in the U.S.	*Since* or *ever since* means "from that time in the past to the present." We use the present perfect or present perfect continuous in the main clause.
While they were taking care of their cattle, their villages were bombed. **As** they were coming to the U.S., they were thinking about their new life ahead.	We use *while* or *as* with a continuous action.
They walked **for** three months. They stayed in a refugee camp **for** many years.	We use *for* with an amount of time.
During the day, they walked. **During** their time in the refugee camp, they studied English.	We use *during* with a time such as *the day* or *summer,* or with a specific time period (*their time in Ethiopia, the month of August*) or an event (*the flight to the U.S.*).

EXERCISE 6 Fill in the blanks with *since, until, while, when, as, during, for,* or *whenever.* In some cases, more than one answer is possible.

1. The Lost Boys were very young ___when___ they left Sudan.
2. The Lost Boys walked ______________ many months.
3. ______________ their march to Ethiopia, many of them died.
4. They lived in Ethiopia ______________ about four years.

258 Lesson 9

TEST/REVIEW

Use the sentence under each blank to form a noun clause. Answers may vary.

Two years ago, when I was eighteen, I didn't know ___what to do___ (1. What should I do?) with my life. I had just graduated from high school, and I couldn't decide ___ (2. Should I go to college or not?). A neighbor of mine told me ___ (3. I had the same problem when I was your age.) and decided to go to the U.S. for a year to work as an au pair. She asked me ___ (4. Have you ever heard of this program?). I told her ___ (5. I haven't.). She told me ___ (6. I lived with an American family for a year.) and ___ (7. My English has improved a lot.). I asked her ___ (8. How much will this program cost me?). I was surprised to find out ___ (9. You'll earn about $200 a week.). I asked her ___ (10. Is the work very hard?), and she said ___ (11. It is.) but ___ (12. It is very rewarding.).

When I told my parents ___ (13. I am thinking about going to the U.S. for a year.), they told me

SUMMARY OF LESSON 10

Direct Statement or Question	Sentence with an Included Statement or Question	Explanation
She loves kids. She is patient.	I know **that she loves kids**. I'm sure **that she is patient**.	A noun clause is used as an included statement.
Is the baby sick? What does the baby need?	I don't know **if the baby is sick**. I'm not sure **what the baby needs**.	A noun clause is used as an included question.
What should I do with a crying baby? Where can I find a babysitter?	I don't know **what to do with a crying baby**. Can you tell me **where to find a babysitter**?	An infinitive can replace *should* or *can*.
You know more than you think you do. Do you have children?	Dr. Spock said, **"You know more than you think you do."** **"Do you have children?"** asked the doctor.	An exact quote is used to report what someone has said or asked.
Do your kids watch Sesame Street? I will teach my son to drive.	She asked me **if my kids watched** Sesame Street. She said **that she would tea[ch] her son to drive**.	A noun clause is used in reported ...
Trust yourself. Don't give the baby candy.	He told us **to trust ourselve[s]** ... He told me **not to give the** ... **candy**.	

Punctuation with Noun Clauses	
I know where he lives.	Period at ...
Do you know where he lives?	Question ... noun clau...
He said, "I like you."	Comma a... Period be...
"I like you," he said.	Quotation ... the final ...
He asked, "What do you want?"	Comma a... quote. Qu...
"What do you want?" he asked.	Quotation ... before th...

PART 2 Editing Practice

Some of the shaded words and phrases have mistakes. Find the mistakes and correct them. If the shaded words are correct, write *C*.

When I was fourteen years old, I told my parents ~~what~~ that (1.) I wanted to work as a babysitter, but they told me (2. C) that (3.) I was too young. At that time, they told me that they will (4.) pay me $1 an hour to help with my little brother. A few times they asked me could I (5.) watch him when they went out. They always told me call (6.) them immediately in case of a problem. They told me don't (7.) watch TV or text my friends while I was working as a babysitter. They always told me that I have (8.) done a good job.

When I was fifteen, I got a few more responsibilities, like preparing small meals. They always told (9.) that (10.) I should teach my brother about good nutrition. I asked them whether I could (11.) get more money because I had more responsibilities, and they agreed. I asked them if I can (12.) buy something new with my earnings. My parents said, (13.) "Of course."

When I turned eighteen, I started working for my neighbors, who have three children. The neighbors asked me had I gotten (14.) my driver's license yet. When I said (15.) yes, they were pleased because I could drive the kids to different places. I never realized how hard was it (16.) to take care of so many kids. As soon as we get in the car, they ask, "Are we there yet?" (17.) They think so (18.) we should arrive immediately. When they're thirsty, they ask me to buy (19.) them soda, but I tell (20.) them what (21.) it is healthier to drink water. They always tell, (22.) "In our house we drink soda." I don't understand why do (23.) their ... w whether to follow (24.) the rules of my house or ... arents told me not to say (26.) anything about their ... lthy habits by example.

... ildren. I hope that I will (28.) be as good a mom to ...

... when you were a child. Explain what the ...

... u or encouraged you when you were a child.

... . Edit your writing from Part 3.

Noun Clauses 313

WRITING

PART 1 Editing Advice

1. Use *that* or nothing to introduce an included statement. Don't use *what*.
   I know ~~what~~ that she is a good driver.
2. Use statement word order in an included question.
   I don't know how fast ~~is he~~ he is driving.
3. We *say* something. We *tell* someone something.
   He ~~said~~ told me that he wanted to go home.
   He ~~told~~ said, "I want to go home."
4. Use *tell* or *ask*, not *say*, to report an imperative. Follow *tell* and *ask* with an object.
   Dr. Spock ~~said~~ told parents to trust themselves.
   My son asked ^me to give him the car keys.
5. Don't use *to* after *tell*.
   She told ~~to~~ me that she wanted to be a teacher.
6. Use *if* or *whether* to introduce an included *yes/no* question. Use statement word order.
   I don't know ^whether teenagers understand the risks while driving.
   I can't decide ~~should I~~ if I should let my daughter get her driver's license.
7. Follow the rule of sequence of tenses when the main verb is in the past.
   Last year my father said that he ~~will~~ would teach me how to drive, but he didn't.
8. Don't use *so* before a noun clause.
   I think ~~so~~ raising children is the best job.
9. Use an infinitive to report an imperative.
   My parents told me ^to drive carefully.
   My parents told me ~~don't~~ not to text while driving.

312 Lesson 10

Enhanced For This Edition!

END-OF-LESSON ACTIVITIES help learners review and apply the target grammar to writing.

Updated For This Edition!

ENHANCED WRITING SECTIONS are divided into two parts which provide students with editing and writing activities to consolidate the grammar structures learned in each lesson.

ADDITIONAL RESOURCES FOR EACH LEVEL

Updated For This Edition!

ONLINE WORKBOOK
powered by MyELT provides students with additional practice of the target grammar and greater flexibility for independent study.

- Engages students and supports classroom materials by providing a variety of interactive grammar activities.
- Tracks course completion through student progress bars, giving learners a sense of personal achievement.
- Supports instructors by maximizing valuable learning time through course management resources, including scheduling and grade reporting tools.

Go to NGL.Cengage.com/MyELT

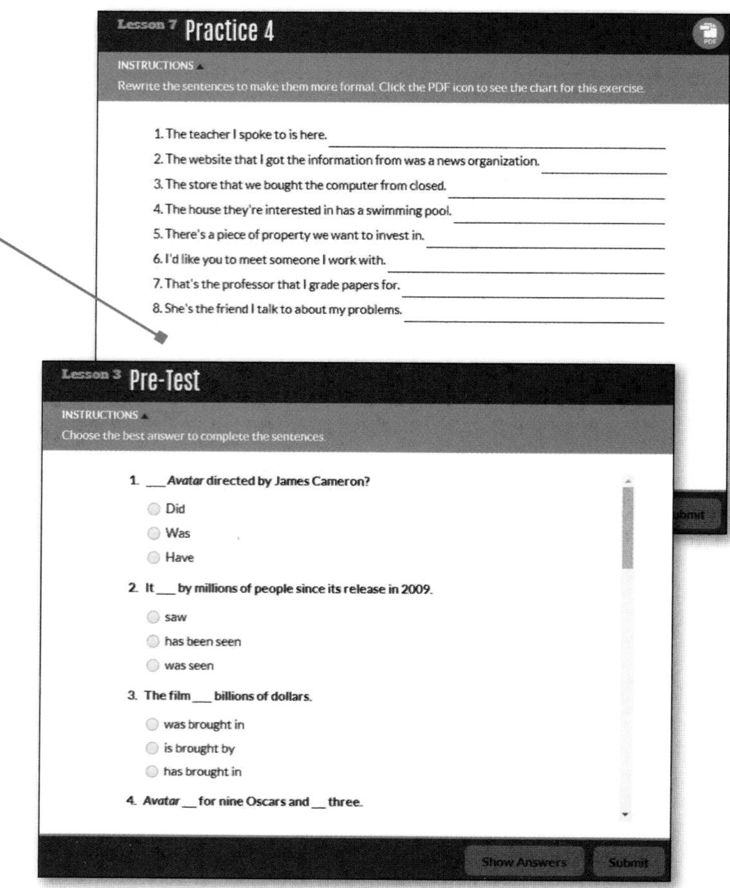

LESSON

7 Adjective Clauses, Descriptive Phrases

ONLINE INTERACTIONS

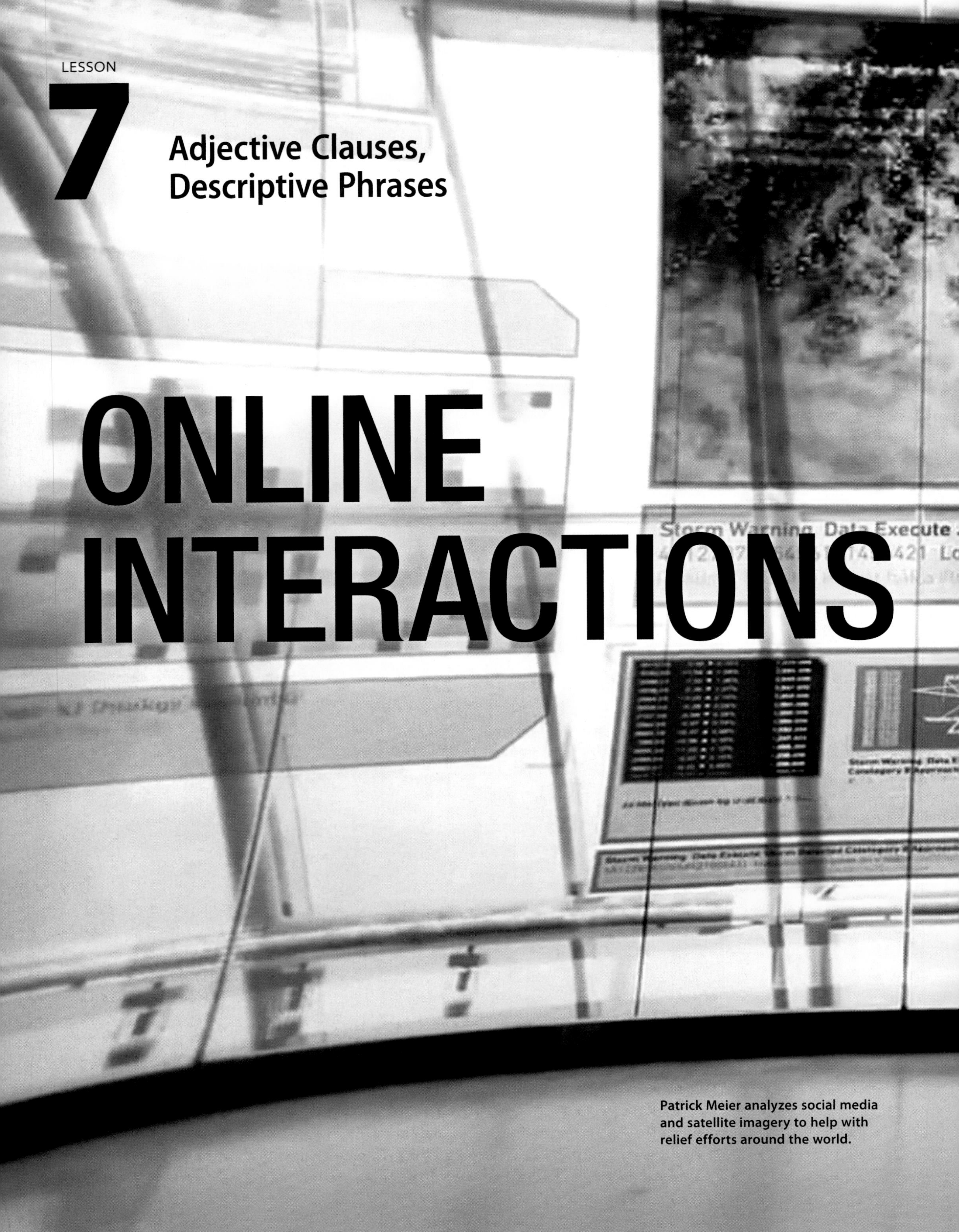

Patrick Meier analyzes social media and satellite imagery to help with relief efforts around the world.

> The dream behind the Web is of a common information space in which we communicate by sharing information. Its universality is essential.
>
> — Tim Berners-Lee

PIERRE OMIDYAR and eBAY

Read the following article. Pay special attention to the words in bold.

Did you ever want to sell a birthday present **that you didn't like**? Or an old toy **that is taking up space in your closet**? In the old days, buyers and sellers were limited to newspapers, garage sales, and flea markets[1] in the area **where they lived**. But in the early 1990s, **when people started to use the Internet**, Pierre Omidyar had an idea. Omidyar, **who was working as a computer programmer**, realized that sellers no longer had to be limited to finding buyers **who lived in their local area**. He came up with the idea of eBay, **which he started as a hobby**. He didn't charge money at first because he wasn't sure eBay would work. Buying online requires you to trust sellers **whom you've never met**. But people liked eBay. Soon there was so much activity on eBay that his Internet service provider upgraded his site to a business account, **which was no longer free**. So Omidyar started to charge the sellers a small fee for each sale. Before long, this hobby grew into a big business.

By 1998, eBay had become so big that Omidyar needed a business expert. He brought in Meg Whitman, **whose knowledge of business helped make eBay a success**. She changed eBay from a company **that sold used things in several categories** to a large marketplace of seventy-eight million items, both new and used, in fifty thousand categories.

Many companies **that start out well on the Internet** later fail. When Whitman left the company, it started to decline. In 2008, John Donahoe was brought in as the new CEO.[2] He fired many people **who had been working there for years**. He understood that smartphones and tablets were changing the way **that people shopped**; people no longer had to shop from their home computers. He created an eBay app so that people could shop 24/7 and could pay with one click. eBay, **which was about to follow other Internet businesses into decline**, was brought back to life.

By the time Omidyar was 31, he was worth more than $7 billion. The money **that he has earned** is much more than he needs. He and his wife signed a promise, the Giving Pledge, to give away the majority of their wealth during their lifetime to help others.

---

1 *flea market:* a market where used items are sold

2 *CEO:* Chief Executive Officer; the highest executive in charge of a company or organization

COMPREHENSION CHECK Based on the reading, tell if the statement is true (**T**) or false (**F**).

1. Omidyar did not start out with the intention of making money.
2. Because of John Donahoe, eBay was starting to fail.
3. Omidyar believes in sharing his wealth.

7.1 Adjective Clauses—Introduction

Examples	Explanation
I received a birthday present **that I didn't like.** You have to trust sellers **whom you've never met.** Omidyar changed to a business account, **which** was not free.	The adjective clause identifies which present. An adjective clause is a group of words that contains a subject and verb. It describes or identifies the noun before it. It is a dependent clause. In these examples, the adjective clauses describe the nouns: *present, sellers*, and *account*.

Language Notes:

1. The following words mark the beginning of an adjective clause: *who, whom, that, which, whose, where, when.*
2. Sometimes an adjective clause begins with no marker.
   I received a birthday present **I didn't like**.
3. Some adjective clauses are set apart from the rest of the sentence by commas.
   John Donahoe saved eBay, **which was declining**.
4. An adjective clause can follow any noun in a sentence.
   The company hired Meg Whitman, **who knew a lot about business**.
   Meg Whitman, **who left the company to go into politics**, helped make eBay a success.

EXERCISE 1 Listen to each sentence and fill in the word that marks the beginning of the adjective clause.

CD 2
TR 3

1. Amazon was founded in 1994 by Jeff Bezos, ____who____ predicted that the Internet offered an opportunity to make money.
2. Amazon, ____________ is now the largest online retailer, began by selling books.
3. First Bezos made a list of about 20 products ____________ could be sold online. He eventually decided on selling books.
4. Bezos wanted a name ____________ began with "A." He decided on Amazon, because it is a place ____________ is "exotic and different."
5. But a good company name is not enough. Bezos needed to hire people ____________ talents would improve the company.

continued

6. Since many big Internet companies started in a garage, Bezos decided to buy a house ________________ had a garage.
7. Bezos needed money to start his company. He went to his parents, ________________ first response was "What's the Internet?"
8. Some people thought that his parents would lose all the money ________________ they invested.
9. His parents, ________________ invested $300,000 in his business, believed in their son's project.
10. The 1990s was a time ________________ people were just beginning to use the Internet.
11. Bezos created a place ________________ customers could make recommendations to other users.
12. Bezos and his parents were never unhappy about the decision ________________ he made in 1994.

EXERCISE 2 Underline the adjective clause in each of these sentences.

1. Amazon was founded in 1994 by Jeff Bezos, <u>who predicted that the Internet offered an opportunity to make money</u>.
2. Amazon, which is now the largest online retailer, began by selling books.
3. First he made a list of about twenty products that could be sold online. He eventually decided on selling books.
4. Bezos wanted a name that began with "A." He decided on Amazon, because it is a place that is "exotic and different."
5. But a good company name is not enough. He needed to hire people whose talents would improve the company.
6. Since many big Internet companies started in a garage, he decided to buy a house that had a garage.
7. He needed money to start his company. He went to his parents, whose first response was "What's the Internet?"
8. Some people thought that his parents would lose all the money that they invested.
9. The 1990s was a time when people were just beginning to use the Internet.
10. Bezos created a place where customers could make recommendations to other users.
11. He and his parents were never unhappy about the decision that he made in 1994.

7.2 Relative Pronoun as Subject

The relative pronouns *who, that,* and *which* can be the subject of the adjective clause.

Subject I want to sell an old toy. *The toy* is in my closet. ↓ I want to sell an old toy **that / which** is in my closet.
The person...lives in another state. **Subject** *The person* bought the toy. ↓ The person **who / that** bought the toy lives in another state.

Language Notes:

1. Use the relative pronouns *who* and *that* for people. Use the relative pronouns *that* and *which* for things.
2. A present-tense verb in the adjective clause must agree in number with its subject.
   People who **buy** things online like the convenience.
   A person who **buys** things online likes the convenience.

EXERCISE 3 Fill in the blanks with *who* or *that* + the correct form of the verb, using the tense given to complete the adjective clauses.

1. I have a friend ___who buys___ (present: buy) all her books online.
2. People ______________ (present: buy) books online can write reviews and give a book 1-5 stars.
3. A person ______________ (present: read) the reviews can be influenced by the opinions of others.
4. There are many neighborhood bookstores ______________ (past: lose) business and had to close because of online competition.
5. There are people ______________ (present perfect: create) successful businesses on the Internet.
6. Omidyar and Bezos are two people ______________ (past: understand) the potential of the Internet.
7. Jeff Bezos is lucky to have parents ______________ (past: believe) in his idea.
8. Friendster and MySpace were two Internet companies ______________ (past: become) successful and then failed.

continued

9. When you buy something online, you often see this: "People ______________ (past: buy) this product also bought...."

10. You are encouraged to buy products ______________ (present: be) similar to your purchase.

11. Pierre Omidyar gives a lot of his money to organizations ______________ (present: help) people in need.

EXERCISE 4 Work with a partner. Write a complete sentence, using the noun + the adjective clause given as the subject or object of your sentence. Write about computers, the Internet, or technology in general.

1. a computer that has little memory

   A computer that has little memory is not useful today. OR

   No one wants a computer that has little memory.

2. students who don't have a computer

   ____

3. children who spend all their time playing computer games

   ____

4. e-mail that comes from an unknown sender

   ____

5. websites that offer music downloads

   ____

6. people who don't know anything about computers

   ____

7. kids who are born into today's world

   ____

8. a flash drive that has 10 MB of memory

   ____

7.3 Relative Pronoun as Object

The relative pronouns *who(m), that,* and *which* can be the object of the adjective clause.

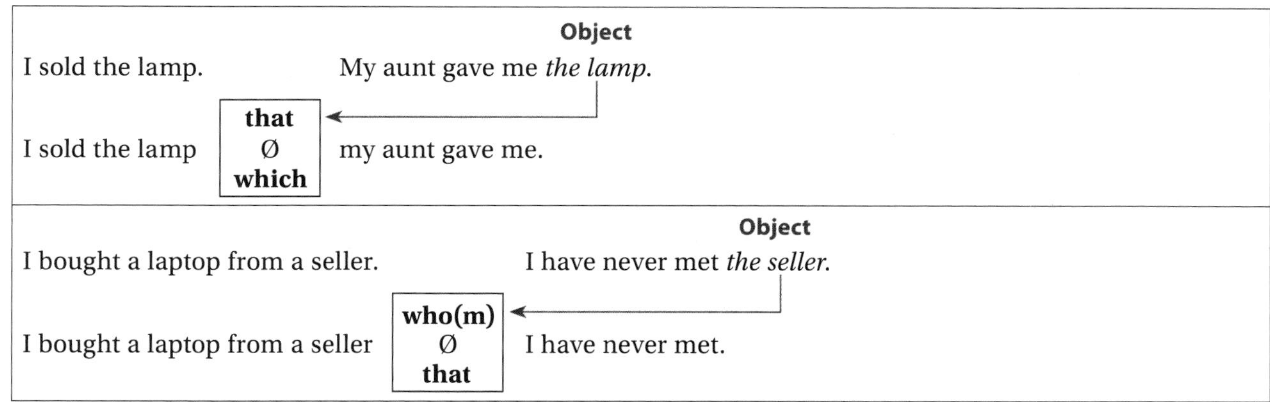

Language Notes:

1. The relative pronoun is usually omitted in conversation when it is the object of the adjective clause.

   I sold the lamp ~~that~~ my aunt gave me.
   I bought a laptop from a seller ~~whom~~ I've never met.

2. *Whom* is considered more formal than *who* when used as the object of the adjective clause. However, as seen in the note above, the relative pronoun is usually omitted altogether in conversation.

   Pierre Omidyar is a man *whom* I greatly admire. (formal)
   Pierre Omidyar is a man *who* OR *that* I greatly admire. (less formal)
   Pierre Omidyar is a man I greatly admire. (informal)

3. When there is no new subject after the relative pronoun, the relative pronoun is the subject of the adjective clause and cannot be omitted.

   My neighborhood has a bookstore **that** has a reading hour for children.

4. When a new subject is introduced in the adjective clause, the relative pronoun is the object of the adjective clause and can be omitted.

   My neighborhood has a bookstore **(that)** the children love.

EXERCISE 5 In the conversations below, use the underlined words and other context clues to help you fill in the blanks with adjective clauses. Answers may vary.

1. **A:** I just bought a new computer.

   B: But didn't you just buy one a year ago?

   A: You're right. But the one ___(that) I bought___ last year is old already.

continued

2. **A:** I'm so tired of all the spam ______________________ (a).

B: What's spam? That's a word ______________________ (b).

A: You don't know the word "spam"? It's junk e-mail. Everyone gets it.

B: I don't get much spam. I have an e-mail address ______________________ (c) just for shopping online. I don't use it for anything else. I often buy shoes online.

A: How do you know if they're going to fit?

B: The shoes ______________________ (d) are always the same, so I don't have to worry about the size. Besides, if I don't want the item, I can return it.

A: Don't you have to pay to send things back?

B: That depends on the company ______________________ (e). If you use certain companies, they offer free returns. You should try online shopping. You can save a lot of time.

A: You prefer that method. But that's not for me. The method ______________________ (f) is driving to a mall, getting exercise by walking into the store, trying on the shoes, and walking back to my car.

B: I don't need exercise walking into a store. I get all the exercise ______________________ (g) with my new running shoes.

3. **A:** Do you want to see a picture of my new girlfriend, Nina?

B: I didn't know you had a new girlfriend. What happened to the last girlfriend ______________________ (a)? Carla, right?

A: Yeah, Carla. She thought I spent too much time taking pictures, texting, and using the Internet. So she broke up with me.

B: I see you still have some pictures of Carla on your phone.

A: Oh, right. I'd better delete the pictures ______________________ (b) of Carla before Nina sees them.

B: Let me give you some advice. You'd better put down your phone and spend more time with Nina.

A: I hope I can follow the advice ______________________ (c) me. If not, I'll lose Nina.

4. **A:** Can I see your new phone? Wow. Look at all the apps ______________ (a.).

B: I know I've got a lot of apps.

A: You must spend a lot of money on new apps.

B: Not really. Most of the apps ______________ (b.) are free.

A: I see you've got a new phone case. It's not as cool as the last one ______________ (c.). Why did you change?

B: This was a gift from my grandmother. It was the present ______________ (d.) me for my birthday. I don't want her to feel hurt. I just wish she'd give me a gift card and let me pick out my own present.

A: I'm sure she meant well.

5. **A:** I found a great site for planning a trip. Owners rent out their houses to vacationers. Look. I'll show it to you.

B: Wow! I see that's a beautiful house with a swimming pool. Does it really look like that?

A: The pictures ______________ (a.) here are pretty accurate. This is the house ______________ (b.) last summer and it was great. The house ______________ (c.) next year is even more beautiful.

B: Why don't you just get a hotel room? What's the advantage of renting a home?

A: The hotel rooms ______________ (d.) in the past were small. By renting a home, we have a kitchen, so we can cook and save money that way.

B: How much does it cost?

A: This one costs $1,500 for the week, plus a security deposit.

B: Wow! $1,500 sounds like a lot of money.

A: We split the money between the number of people in our group. And the more friends ______________ (e.) to go with us, the cheaper it'll be.

B: If you can't find anyone else, I'll go with you!

7.4 Relative Pronoun as Object of Preposition

The relative pronoun can be the object of a preposition (*to, about, with, of,* etc.).

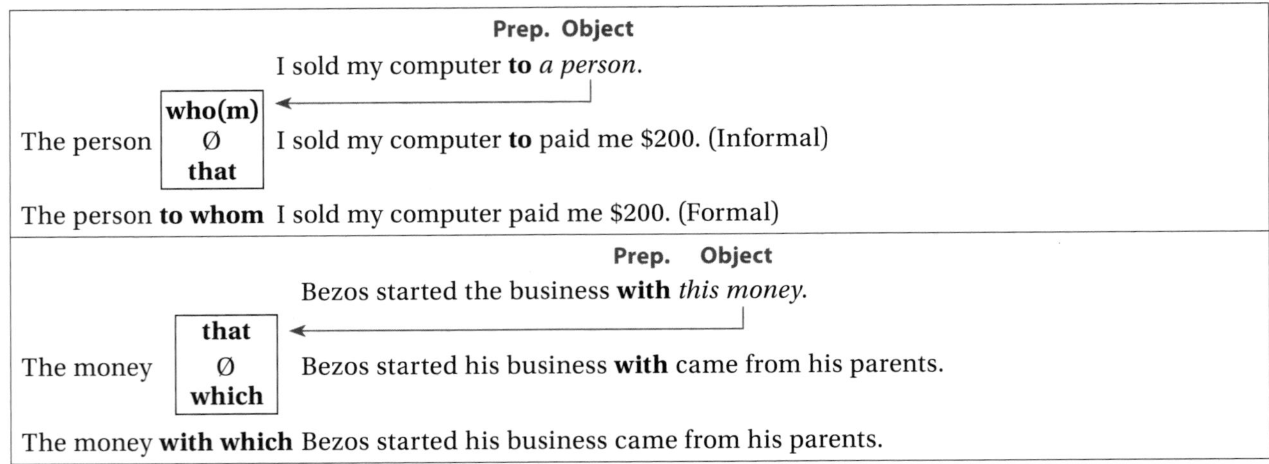

Prep. Object

I sold my computer **to** *a person*.

The person **who(m)** / Ø / **that** I sold my computer **to** paid me $200. (Informal)

The person **to whom** I sold my computer paid me $200. (Formal)

Prep. Object

Bezos started the business **with** *this money*.

The money **that** / Ø / **which** Bezos started his business **with** came from his parents.

The money **with which** Bezos started his business came from his parents.

Language Notes:

1. The relative pronouns can be the object of a preposition (*to, about, with, of,* etc.).
2. Informally, most native speakers put the preposition at the end of the adjective clause. The relative pronoun is usually omitted.
   The person I sold my computer **to** paid me $200.
   Do you know the person you bought your laptop **from**?
3. In formal English, the preposition comes before the relative pronoun, and only *whom* and *which* may be used. *That* is not used directly after a preposition.
   The person **to whom** I sold my computer paid me $200. (NOT: *to who* or *to that*)
   The money **with which** Bezos started his business came from his parents. (NOT: *to that*)

EXERCISE 6 Make these sentences more informal by taking out the relative pronoun and putting the preposition at the end of the adjective clause.

1. There are several travel websites in which I am interested.
   There are several travel websites I'm interested in.
2. There is a new website about which everyone is talking.
   ____
3. The link on which you click will take you to that site.
   ____
4. The information for which you are looking can be found on that site.
   ____

5. Vacation Rentals is not a website with which I'm familiar.

____

6. Finding a vacation home online is not a method to which I'm accustomed.

____

7. The house on which we decided is in the mountains.

____

8. The owner to whom I spoke was very helpful.

____

9. There's one thing about which I'm sure: renting a vacation home is a good deal.

____

EXERCISE 7 Combine the two sentences to make one. Write each sentence in the formal and informal way starting with the words given.

1. This site has vacation rentals. I'm interested in these vacation rentals.

   This site has vacation rentals (which/that) I'm interested in.

   This site has vacation rentals in which I'm interested.

2. I'm interested in a house. The house has three bedrooms.

   The house ____

   The house ____

3. I'm taking a vacation with some friends. These friends want to rent a house.

   The friends ____

   The friends ____

4. I got a lot of information from a person. I spoke to the person.

   I got a lot of information from the person ___________________________

   I got a lot of information from the person ___________________________

5. We are responsible for only one thing. We are responsible for cleaning the house.

   The only thing ____

   The only thing ____

The FREECYCLE NETWORK™

Read the following article. Pay special attention to the words in bold.

CD 2 TR 4

Do you have an old computer that you don't need anymore? Or are you trying to find an extra TV but don't want to spend money? Then The Freecycle Network is for you. The name combines the word "free" and the word "recycle." The Freecycle Network is an online community **whose** members help each other get what they need—for free! Unlike eBay, Freecycle is a geographical community. You join in the area **where** you live.

Americans generate almost five pounds of garbage per person per day. About 55 percent of this garbage is buried in what is called "landfill." Buried garbage can cause environmental problems. This garbage often contains useful items that other people may need.

The Freecycle Network was created in 2003 by Deron Beal, **whose** idea was to protect the environment by keeping usable goods out of landfill. He also wanted to encourage neighbors to help each other. He started his network in Tucson, Arizona, **where** he lives. He sent an e-mail to about thirty or forty friends to see if they wanted to join. His Freecycle community grew quickly. Today there are more than seven million members in over five thousand groups around the world. The Freecycle Network reports that its members are keeping five hundred tons of goods out of landfill each day.

Artist Mike Stilkey uses discarded books to create art pieces.

How do members deliver or receive the item? The person **whose** offered item you want will let you know the place **where** you can pick it up. Very often, the item will be left in front of the giver's house for the receiver. The giver will specify a time **when** the receiver can pick up the item. Sometimes the giver and receiver will meet.

It's always important to be polite. You should always send a thank-you e-mail to the person **whose** item you received.

COMPREHENSION CHECK Based on the reading, tell if the statement is true (**T**) or false (**F**).

1. Users of Freecycle sometimes have to send packages to other cities.
2. Unwanted items are often buried in landfill.
3. Freecycle is similar to eBay.

7.5 Place and Time in Adjective Clauses

Examples	Explanation
The city **where** I live has a recycling group. The city **in which** I live has a recycling group. The city **(that)** I live **in** has a recycling group.	We can express place in an adjective clause with: • *where* to mean "in that place." • a preposition + *which*. (formal) • *that/which* or Ø + clause + preposition.
Please decide on a time period **(when)** you can pick up the item. Please decide on a time period **during which** you can pick up the item.	We can express time in an adjective clause with: • *when* or Ø. • a preposition + *which*. (formal)
My front door is the place **where** I leave packages for others. My front door is the place **that** shows my address. The 1990s was a time **when** the Internet was new. The 1990s was a decade **that** I don't remember well. I was just a small child.	*Where* means in *that place* or *there*. (I leave packages there.) *That* refers to the noun that precedes it. (The place shows my address.) *When* means *at that time* or *then*. (The Internet was new then.) *That* refers to the noun that precedes it. (I don't remember that decade.)

EXERCISE 8 Circle the correct words to complete the conversation. In some cases, both choices are correct, so circle both options.

A: Grandma, I can't imagine a time (*when/where*) there were no computers.
1.

B: It wasn't such a long time ago. When I was in high school, we had never seen a computer. We used typewriters to write our papers. There was a special room in my school (*where/that*) you could go and use the typewriters.
2.

A: You mean like a computer lab?

B: Something like that. Later I read a book about computers, and I wanted to know more. At the time (*Ø/when*) I first became interested in computers, I didn't know anyone who had one.
3.

continued

A: Did you buy your computer online?

B: Oh, no. I'm talking about a time (*when/about which*) no one had even heard of the Internet. There were
4.
very few stores (*Ø/where*) you could buy computers. And they were so expensive.
5.

A: More than $500?

B: More than $2,000!

A: Wow! It must have had a big memory.

B: Absolutely not. I'm talking about a time (*when/that*) 100 kilobytes was considered a big memory. The
6.
computer tower was very big. I had to find a place under my desk (*that/where*) I could put the tower.
7.

A: Who taught you to use it?

B: I had to find a time (*which/when*) I could study on my own because I had no one to help me. Later
8.
I started taking a class at a community college near my house. Did you know that there was a time (*Ø/when*) most computer students were guys? I was the only woman in the class.
9.

A: Grandma. I'm so proud of you. What happened to your first computer?

B: For many years, it was in my garage. Then I decided to put it on a website (*where/that*) people go in
10.
order to buy old computers.

A: Why would anyone want such an old computer?

B: There are collectors who consider my first computer a collector's item.

A: Cool. So, Grandma, you were ahead of your time.

B: I guess I was. But now, when I have a computer question, I have to ask my grandchildren. It's just hard to find a time (*when/where*) you're not too busy to give your old grandma some help.
11.

EXERCISE 9 About You Write the name of three websites you use frequently. Tell what a person can find on these websites. Share your answers with a partner.

1. Weather.com is a site where you can find out the weather in your area.
2. CCC.edu is a site that has a listing of college courses in Chicago.
3. ______________________________

4. ____

5. ____

EXERCISE 10 About You Write three years or time periods. Tell what happened at that time. Share your answers with a partner.

1. 2012 was the year (when) I got married.
2. December 22 through January 5 were the weeks during which we had our winter break.
3. ____
4. ____
5. ____

7.6 *Whose* in Adjective Clauses

Whose is the possessive form of *who*. It stands for *his, her, its, their,* or the possessive form of the noun.

Whose + noun can be the subject of the adjective clause.

Freecycle is an online community. ***Its* members** help each other. (Subject: *Its* members)

Freecycle is an online community ***whose* members help each other**.

People can offer their kids' old clothes. ***Their* children** are growing. (Subject: *Their* children)

People ***whose* children are growing** can offer their kids' old clothes.

Whose + noun can be the object of the adjective clause.

You should always thank the person. You received ***her* item**. (Object: *her* item)

You should always thank the person ***whose* item you received**.

You want ***a person's* item**. The person will suggest a way for you to get it. (Object: *a person's* item)

The person ***whose* item you want** will suggest a way for you to get it.

EXERCISE 11 Suppose you find these sentences on a recycling site. Write one sentence using *whose* to tell what each person needs or offers to give away.

1. "My basement was flooded. I need new furniture."

   A person whose basement was flooded needs new furniture.

2. "My radio broke. I need a new one."

   ____

3. "My daughter needs a violin. She's in the school orchestra."

   ____

4. "My bicycle was stolen. I need one to get to work.

   ____

5. "My new apartment is small. I want to give away a lot of books."

   ____

6. "My laptop doesn't work anymore. I need a new one."

   ____

7. "My children are grown now. I want to give away their toys."

   ____

8. "My kids are starting school. I need two backpacks."

   ____

EXERCISE 12 Use the sentence given to form an adjective with *whose*.

1. The person whose tablet I bought wanted to get the latest model.
   I bought this person's tablet.
2. The person ______________________ was very helpful.
   I found this person's vacation rental online.
3. The person ______________________ didn't charge me for shipping.
   I bought this person's computer online.
4. I have a friend on a social media site ______________________.
   I don't like this person's profile picture.
5. The person ______________________ is an old friend of mine.
   I received her picture by e-mail.
6. I need to re-enter the e-mail addresses of people ______________________.
   I accidentally deleted their names.
7. The person ______________________ is my best friend.
   You see his picture on my page.
8. The teacher ______________________ has a course website.
   We're taking this teacher's class.

7.7 Adjective Clauses after Indefinite Pronouns

Examples	Explanation
Everyone **who sells on eBay** has to pay a fee. I know someone **who always shops online**.	The relative pronoun after an indefinite pronoun (*someone, something, everyone, everything, no one, nothing, anything*) can be the subject of the adjective clause. The relative pronoun cannot be omitted.
No one wanted anything **(that) I posted online**. Almost everyone **(that/who/whom) I know** has posted a photo online.	The relative pronoun after an indefinite pronoun can be the object of the adjective clause. In this case, it is usually omitted.

EXERCISE 13 Fill in the blanks with an adjective clause. Use the underlined verb to help you. Use the correct verb tense.

1. **A:** I know you've gotten a lot of things online. How has that worked out for you?

   B: I'm happy with everything (that) I have gotten online.

2. **A:** Do you need to buy anything for your new apartment?

   B: Not anymore. I found almost everything ______________________ for free on Freecycle..

3. **A:** I heard you've bought a lot of things online.

   B: So far, everything ______________________ has been great.

continued

4. **A:** My mother still uses a flip phone. Can you believe it?

   B: I don't know anyone ______________________ a flip phone anymore. Everyone
   (a.)

   ______________________ uses a smartphone.
   (b.)

   A: I know one person who doesn't use a cell phone at all—my grandpa.

5. **A:** I sent you an e-mail about vacation rentals. Did you get it?

   B: I didn't see anything ______________________ me about vacation rentals. Oh, wait. Now I see it.

6. **A:** Something ______________________ me about this shopping website was very important, but I forgot it.

   B: I told you that this site offers free shipping.

7. **A:** I saw the beautiful pictures of your vacation rental online. Were the pictures accurate?

   B: The house was exactly like everything ______________________ in the pictures. Maybe the house was even prettier.

8. **A:** I heard you can rent a vacation home online. Do you have to pay a security deposit?

   B: Yes. Everyone ______________________ this house has to pay a security deposit.

9. **A:** Do you want to spend money on a new bicycle or get a used one for free?

   B: I don't know anyone ______________________ to spend money when you can get something for free.

10. **A:** Grandma. You should have a social media account. You can communicate with all your friends that way

    B: I don't know anyone my age ______________________ a social media account. People my age prefer to pick up the phone and talk.

TIM BERNERS-LEE

CD 2 TR 5

Read the following article. Pay special attention to the words in bold.

Amazon, Google, eBay ... it was not so long ago that these websites did not exist. These sites, **which are common names for us today**, were made possible because of the vision of one person: Tim Berners-Lee. Berners-Lee is not famous like Bill Gates, **who created Microsoft**, or Steve Jobs, **whose name is easily associated with Apple computers**. Berners-Lee is the creator of the World Wide Web.

Berners-Lee was born in England in 1955, **when the computer was still a new invention**. His parents, **whom he credits with giving him his love of learning**, helped design the first commercially available computer.

In 1980, Berners-Lee was working as a software engineer at a physics laboratory in Switzerland, **where he worked with scientists from around the world**. He thought it was important for these scientists to continue sharing their knowledge once they returned home. He found a way to make this possible through the Web.

In 1990, Berners-Lee introduced the first Web page and the first browser.[3] With the Web he said, "any person could share information with anyone else, anywhere." He made the Web available for free.

Many people confuse the Web with the Internet, **which was designed in the 1970s and was already being used to send information**. The Internet connects computers with cables. The Web connects information with links. According to Berners-Lee, "The Web made the net useful because people are really interested in information (not to mention knowledge and wisdom!) and don't really want to have to know about computers and cables."

As people started to discover how easy it was to find information through these links, the number of Internet users started to grow quickly. Soon businesses found ways of making money by using Web technology.

In 1999, Berners-Lee published a book called *Weaving the Web*, **in which he answers questions he is often asked**: "What were you thinking when you invented the Web?" "What do you think of it now?" "Where is the Web going to take us in the future?" A lot of people want to know if he's sorry that he made the Web free and didn't profit from it; his answer is no.

The Web has been such an important creation that some people compare Berners-Lee to Johann Gutenberg, **who made books possible by inventing moveable type in the fifteenth century**.

---

[3] *browser:* a computer program that provides access to websites on the Internet

COMPREHENSION CHECK Based on the reading, tell if the statement is true (**T**) or false (**F**).

1. Berners-Lee made a lot of money from creating the Web.
2. The Internet and the Web are the same.
3. Berners-Lee learned a lot about computers from his parents.

7.8 Nonessential Adjective Clauses

Examples	Explanation
Berners-Lee is not famous like Bill Gates, **who created Microsoft**. His parents, **whom he admired**, designed computers. The Internet, **which was designed in the 1970s,** connected computers.	Some adjective clauses are not essential to the meaning of the sentence. A nonessential adjective clause adds extra information. The sentence is complete without it.
Berners-Lee worked in Switzerland, **where he shared ideas with other scientists.** In 1990, **when many people had never heard of the Internet,** Berners-Lee created the first Web page. Most people have heard of Steve Jobs, **whose name is easily associated with Apple computers.**	A nonessential adjective clause is separated by commas from the main part of the sentence. A nonessential adjective clause begins with *who, whom, which, where, when,* or *whose. That* is not used in a nonessential adjective clause.

EXERCISE 14 Put commas in the following sentences to separate the nonessential adjective clause from the main clause.

1. The first modern computer, which was called ENIAC, took up a lot of space.
2. ENIAC was created in 1942 when the U.S. was involved in World War II.
3. Personal computers which were introduced in the 1970s were smaller and faster than previous computers.
4. Berners-Lee whose name is not widely recognized made a great contribution to the world.
5. Bill Gates went to Harvard University where he developed the programming language BASIC.
6. Bill Gates dropped out of Harvard to work with Paul Allen who was his old high school friend.
7. Bill Gates and his wife Melinda set up the Bill and Melinda Gates Foundation which helps people in need all over the world.
8. Jeff Bezos got money from his parents who lent him $300,000 to start Amazon.

7.9 Essential vs. Nonessential Adjective Clauses

Examples	Explanation
Berners-Lee, **whose parents helped design the first computer**, loved mathematics. Berners-Lee works at MIT, **where he is a professor of engineering**.	In these examples the adjective clause is nonessential because, without it, we can still identify the noun in the main clause. Try reading the sentences without the adjective clause. The sentences are complete. The adjective clause adds extra information to the sentence.
Smartphones changed the way **(that) people shop**. Jeff Bezos wanted a company name **that began with A**. People **who want quick information** can use the Web.	In these examples the adjective clause is essential, because, without it, we can't identify the noun. If we take the adjective clause out, the noun isn't properly identified and the idea isn't complete.
(a) Berners-Lee, **who invented the Web**, is very creative and intelligent. b) The computer, **which was invented in the 1940s**, has become part of our everyday lives. (c) The computer **that I bought two years ago** is slow compared to today's computers.	In example (a), Berners-Lee is unique and does not need to be identified. The clause is nonessential. Example (b) refers to the whole class of computers as an invention. The clause is nonessential. Example (c) refers to only one computer, which is identified by the adjective clause. The clause is essential.
The computer ***(that)*** **she just bought** has a lot of memory. The Web, ***which*** **Berners-Lee created**, is a useful tool.	In an essential adjective clause, the relative pronoun *that* can be used or omitted. In a nonessential adjective clause, the relative pronoun *that* cannot be used. The relative pronoun cannot be omitted.

Language Notes:

Here are some questions to help you decide if the adjective clause needs commas. If the answer to any of these questions is *yes*, then the adjective clause is set off by commas.

- Can I put the adjective clause in parentheses?

  Google **(which is a popular search engine)** was created in 1998.
- Can I write the adjective clause as a separate sentence?

  Google is a popular search engine. **It was created in 1998**.
- If the adjective clause is deleted, does the sentence still make sense?

  Google is a popular search engine.
- Is the noun a unique person, place, or thing?

  Berners-Lee, who works at MIT, invented the Web.
- If the noun is plural, am I including all members of a group?

  Personal computers, **which became popular in the 1990s**, have changed the way we get information. (all personal computers)

EXERCISE 15 Decide which of the following sentences contain a nonessential adjective clause. Put commas in those sentences. If the sentence doesn't need commas, write *NC*.

1. People who text use abbreviations. NC
2. My father, who texted me a few minutes ago, is sick.
3. Kids who spend a lot of time on the computer don't get much exercise.
4. The Freecycle Network™ which was created in 2003 helps keep things out of landfills.
5. People usually have a lot of things they don't need.
6. Berners-Lee whose parents were very educated loves learning new things.
7. At first Amazon was a company that only sold books.
8. Meg Whitman who ran eBay for ten years left the company in 2008.
9. Berners-Lee worked in Switzerland where a physics laboratory is located.
10. The Windows operating system which was developed by Microsoft came out in 1985.
11. Did you like the story that we read about Berners-Lee?
12. The computer that I bought three years ago doesn't have enough memory.
13. The Web which is one of the most important inventions of the twentieth century has changed the way people get information.
14. Bill Gates who created Microsoft with his friend became a billionaire.
15. Steve Jobs who died in 2011 helped create the Apple computer.
16. It's hard to remember a time when computers were not part of our everyday lives.
17. Do you remember the year when you bought your first computer?

EXERCISE 16 Combine the two sentences into one. The sentence in parentheses ( ) is not essential to the main idea of the sentence. It adds extra information.

1. eBay is now a large corporation. (It was started in Pierre Omidyar's house.)

   eBay, which was started in Pierre Omidyar's house, is now a large corporation.

2. Tim Berners-Lee works at MIT. (He does research on artificial intelligence there.)

   ____

3. Pierre Omidyar started eBay as a hobby. (His wife became part of the company.)

   ____

4. eBay hired Meg Whitman in 1998. (More expert business knowledge was needed at that time to run the company.)

   ____

5. In 2008, eBay hired John Donahoe. (He fired a lot of people.)

   ____

6. E-mail did not become popular until the 1990s. (It was first created in 1972.)

____

7. Pierre Omidyar had to charge money for each sale. (His idea started to become popular.)

____

8. Berners-Lee created the Web at a laboratory in Switzerland. (He was working there in the 1980s.)

____

9. Berners-Lee wrote a book called *Weaving the Web.* (He answers questions about his project in this book.)

____

7.10 Descriptive Phrases

Examples	Explanation
(a) There are millions of items **that are listed on eBay**. (b) There are millions of items **listed on eBay**.	Compare sentence (a) with an adjective clause to sentence (b) with a descriptive phrase. This descriptive phrase begins with a past participle.
(a) I sold some things **that were taking up space in my closet**. (b) I sold some things **taking up space in my closet**.	Compare sentence (a) with an adjective clause to sentence (b) with a descriptive phrase. This descriptive phrase begins with a present participle (verb *-ing*).
(a) Pierre Omidyar, **who is the founder of eBay**, is one of the richest men in the world. (b) Pierre Omidyar, **the founder of eBay**, is one of the richest men in the world.	Compare sentence (a) with an adjective clause to sentence (b) with a descriptive phrase. This descriptive phrase is a noun (phrase). It gives a definition or more information about the preceding noun. This kind of descriptive phrase is called an appositive.
(a) Pierre Omidyar, **who is from France**, created eBay. (b) Pierre Omidyar, **from France**, created eBay.	Compare sentence (a) with an adjective clause to sentence (b) with a descriptive phrase. This descriptive phrase begins with a preposition (*with, in, from, of,* etc.).

Language Notes:

1. We can only shorten an adjective clause to a descriptive phrase if the relative pronoun is followed by the verb *be.*

   I often use the computers ~~that are~~ in the library.

2. A descriptive phrase can be essential or nonessential. A nonessential phrase is set off by commas.

   I have two computers. The computer **in my bedroom** is newer. (Essential)

   The Amazon office, **in Seattle,** has over 100,000 employees. (Nonessential)

3. An appositive is always nonessential.

   Amazon, **an online store**, is a very popular website.

EXERCISE 17 Shorten the adjective clause to a descriptive phrase by crossing out the unnecessary words.

1. On eBay, people ~~who are~~ living in California can easily sell to people ~~who are~~ living in New York.
2. Google, which is a popular search engine, is used by millions of people.
3. Bill Gates, who is the founder of Microsoft, has set up a foundation to help others.
4. eBay takes a percentage of each sale that is made on its website.
5. Tim Berners-Lee, who is from England, now works at MIT.
6. MIT, which is located in Massachusetts, is an excellent university.
7. Berners-Lee developed the idea for the Web when he was working at CERN, which is a physics lab in Switzerland.
8. Berners-Lee's parents worked on the first computer that was sold commercially.
9. People who are interested in reading newspapers from other cities can find them on the Web.
10. The World Wide Web, which is abbreviated WWW, was first introduced on the Internet in 1991.
11. The Internet, which was designed in the 1970s, didn't attract casual users until Berners-Lee created the Web.
12. Some wealthy people signed a Giving Pledge, which is a promise to give away most of their money in their lifetime.
13. Pierre Omidyar, who is a billionaire, signed the Giving Pledge.
14. Computers that are sold today have much more memory and speed than computers that were sold ten years ago.
15. Deron Beal, who is from Arizona, created The Freecycle Network™.

EXERCISE 18 Combine the two sentences into one sentence. Use the second sentence as the adjective clause or descriptive phrase. (The second sentence adds nonessential information.)

1. Pierre Omidyar came to the U.S. when he was a child. His father was a professor.

   Pierre Omidyar, whose father was a professor, came to the U.S. when he was a child.

2. Pierre Omidyar wrote his first computer program at age 14. He is from France.

   ____

3. He lived in California. He started his business there.

   ____

4. Pierre Omidyar saw a good use for computer technology. He started eBay as a hobby in his home.

   ____

5. *BusinessWeek* named Meg Whitman among the 25 most powerful business managers. *BusinessWeek* is a popular business magazine.

   ____

6. Meg Whitman resigned from eBay in 2008. She decided to go into politics at that time.

   ____

7. John Donahoe got the company out of decline. Pierre Omidyar hired him in 2008.

____

8. Bill Gates started Microsoft at the age of 19. He dropped out of Harvard during his second year.

____

9. Amazon began by selling books. It is now the largest online retailer.

____

10. Jeff Bezos's parents invested money in Amazon. They had never heard of the Internet.

____

11. Tim Berners-Lee is sometimes compared to Johann Gutenberg. Gutenberg made books possible in the fifteenth century.

____

12. Berners-Lee was interested in using the Internet to share information. His parents designed computers.

____

EXERCISE 19 About You Fill in the blanks. Discuss your answers with a partner.

1. ______________________ is one thing I don't like about computers.
2. ______________________ is a website I recommend because ______________________.
3. ______________________, a website young people use a lot, is not so popular with older people.
4. In this lesson, I especially liked the story we read about ______________________ because ______________________.
5. The story we read about Tim Berners-Lee surprised me because ______________________.

SUMMARY OF LESSON 7

	Essential Adjective Clauses	Nonessential Adjective Clauses
Pronoun as subject	People **who/that sell on eBay** have to pay a fee. Amazon is a website **that/which sells a lot of different things**.	Berners-Lee, **who created the Web**, didn't make money from it. Pierre Omidyar created eBay, **which helps people buy and sell items online**.
Pronoun as object	The people **(who/whom) Omidyar hired** helped him build his company. The first computer **(that/which) I bought** didn't have much memory.	Pierre Omidyar, **who(m) I admire**, believes in donating money to help others. I'm very happy with my present computer, **which** I bought online.
Pronoun as object of preposition	INFORMAL: The person **(who/that) I sold my computer to** paid me $200. FORMAL: The person **to whom I sold my computer** paid me $200.	INFORMAL: Berners-Lee, **who(m) we read about**, is very creative. FORMAL: Berners-Lee, **about whom we read**, is very creative.
Where	I want to go to a college **where I can study computer science**.	Berners-Lee worked in Switzerland, **where he met other scientists**.
When	My grandparents grew up at a time **when there were no personal computers**.	The Web was created in 1991, **when most people did not have personal computers**.
Whose + noun as subject	Freecycle is a community **whose members help each other**.	Berners-Lee, **whose parents worked on computers**, learned a lot about technology when he was young.
Whose + noun as object	I sent a thank-you e-mail to the person **whose radio I received through Freecycle**.	Meg Whitman, **whose business expertise Omidyar needed**, started to work at eBay in 1998.
Adjective clause after indefinite compound	I don't know anyone **who doesn't have a cell phone**. Everything **(that/which) I've learned about the Internet** is fascinating.	
Descriptive phrase	Computers **made in the 1980s** had a very small memory.	Bill Gates, **the founder of Microsoft**, never finished college.

TEST/REVIEW

PART 1 Circle the correct words to complete the sentences. Ø means no word is necessary. In some cases, more than one answer is possible. If so, circle all possible answers.

1. What is a computer virus? A virus is a computer code (*that/who/whose/which*) attaches itself to other programs and causes harm to programs, data, or hardware.
2. Who is Deron Beal? Deron Beal is the man (*who/whom/which/that*) created the Freecycle Network.
3. Tim Berners-Lee was born at a time (*when/that/which/Ø*) personal computers were not even in people's imaginations.
4. Tim Berners-Lee is a name (*which/with which/that/Ø*) people are not familiar.
5. Omidyar needed to bring in someone (*who/whose/that/which*) knowledge of business was greater than his own.
6. The Web is a tool (*Ø/that/about which/which*) most of us use every day.
7. The Web, (*which/that/about which/about that*) we read on page 199, is not the same as the Internet.
8. What is eBay? eBay is a website (*that/where/whom/which*) you can buy and sell items.
9. The people (*Ø/which/whose/where*) I've met in online recycling sites have been very helpful.
10. Do you save all the e-mails (*that/where/whose/Ø*) your friends have sent to you?
11. The computer lab is never open at a time (*which/where/when/during which*) I need it.
12. I always delete the spam (*what/that/when/whose*) I receive.
13. You can create an address book (*when/that/where/in which*) you can keep the e-mail addresses of your contacts.
14. Do you know anyone (*Ø/who/whom/which*) doesn't own a computer?
15. The person (*who/that/whose/Ø*) computer I bought wanted a much more powerful computer.
16. Don't believe everything (*that/who/whom/Ø*) you read on the Internet.

PART 2 Some of the following sentences need commas. If they do, put them in. If the sentence doesn't need commas, write *NC* (no commas).

1. John Donahoe, who replaced Meg Whitman, saved eBay from decline.
2. In 2008 when John Donahoe came to work at eBay many top employees were fired.
3. Many online businesses that do well in the beginning later fail.
4. Amazon an online retailer was created by Jeff Bezos.
5. At first Amazon was a place where you could buy only books.
6. Now Amazon is a retailer that sells almost anything.
7. I can't remember a time when there were no smartphones.
8. Berners-Lee is a name that most people don't recognize.
9. Everything that we read in this lesson is related to the Internet.
10. Many people confuse the Web with the Internet which was created in the 1970s.
11. There are many websites where you can get travel information.

WRITING

PART 1 Editing Advice

1. Never use *what* as a relative pronoun.

who
I bought a used computer from a person ~~what~~ lives in another state.

that or Ø
Everything ~~what~~ we learned about the Internet is interesting.

2. You can't omit a relative pronoun that is the subject of the adjective clause.

who
I have a cousin ^ doesn't have a computer.

3. If the relative pronoun is the object of the adjective clause, don't put an object after the verb.

The software that I bought ~~it~~ online was very useful.

4. Make sure you use subject-verb agreement in the adjective clause.

s
I have a friend who use^ e-mail a lot.

5. Put a noun before an adjective clause.

A person who
^ ~~Who~~ doesn't know how to use a computer in today's world is lost.

6. Don't confuse *whose* with *who's*.

whose
The person ~~who's~~ computer I bought didn't charge for shipping.

7. Put the subject before the verb in an adjective clause.

my grandfather uses
The computer that ~~uses my grandfather~~ is very old.

8. Use *whose*, not *his*, *her*, or *their* to show possession in an adjective clause.

whose
I have a friend ~~who his~~ knowledge of programming is very advanced.

PART 2 Editing Practice

Some of the shaded words and phrases have mistakes. Find the mistakes and correct them. If the shaded words are correct, write *C*.

Last semester I took a photo editing class that (1. C) has helped me a lot. The teacher ~~what~~ (2. who) taught the class is an expert in photo editing. This teacher, whose name (3.) is Mark Ryan, is patient, helpful, and fun. A lot of the photos I took (4.) were too dark. I learned how to lighten the parts needed (5.) lightening without lightening the whole photo. I also learned to cut out parts I don't want them (6.). For example, I have a family picture, but it has one person who's (7.) not in the family. It's a woman who live (8.) next door to us. She came right at the time when was taking the picture my friend (9.) and she wanted to be in it.

It's a great photo, except for her. I tried scanning it and editing it at home, but I didn't do a good job. My teacher, who his (10.) scanner is much better than mine, scanned the photo and showed me how to cut the neighbor out. I learned many things in this class. Everything what (11.) I learned is very helpful.

I started to take another photo class this semester. The teacher who's class I'm taking (12.) now is not as good as last semester's teacher. Who (13.) wants to learn a lot about photo editing should take Mark Ryan's class.

PART 3 Write About It

1. Write about the ways computers and the Internet have made life simpler.
2. Write about two websites or apps that you like. Explain how they are helpful or enjoyable for you.

PART 4 Edit Your Writing

Reread the Summary of Lesson 7 and the editing advice. Edit your writing from Part 3.

LESSON

8 Infinitives and Gerunds

Rescue professionals in a mountain air rescue training exercise

HELPING OTHERS

Remember that the happiest people are not those getting more, but those giving more.

—H. Jackson Brown Jr.

ANDREW CARNEGIE, PHILANTHROPIST[1]

Read the following article. Pay special attention to the words in bold.

CD 2
TR 6

Andrew Carnegie was one of the world's richest men. He made a fortune[2] in the oil and steel industries. Did he enjoy his wealth? Of course, he did. But there is something he enjoyed even more: giving away his money.

Carnegie was born in Scotland in 1835 to a very poor family. When his father lost his job, his mother started **to work** to support the family. When Andrew was thirteen years old, his mother persuaded his father **to leave** Scotland for the "possibilities of America." A year later, Andrew started **to work** in a factory in Pittsburgh. He met a man who let him and other working boys use his small library. Andrew was eager **to read** and **learn** as much as he could. He was intelligent and hardworking, and it didn't take him long **to become** rich.

As Carnegie's fortunes grew, he started **to give** his money away. One of his biggest desires was **to build** free public libraries. He wanted everyone **to have** access to libraries and education. He believed that education was the key to a successful life. In 1881, there were only a few public libraries. Carnegie started **to build** free libraries so that everyone would have access to knowledge. Over the doors of the Carnegie Library of Pittsburgh, carved in stone, are the words, "Free to the People." By the time Carnegie died in 1919, there were more than 2,500 public libraries in the English-speaking world.

But building libraries was not his only contribution. In his book *The Gospel of Wealth,* he tried **to persuade** other wealthy people **to give** away their money. These are some of the ideas he wrote about in his book:

- **To give** away money is the best thing rich people can do.
- It is the moral obligation of the wealthy **to help** others.
- It is important for a rich person **to set** an example for others.
- It is not good **to have** money if your spirit is poor.
- It is a disgrace[3] **to die** rich.

By the time he died, Carnegie had given away more than $350 million.[4]

---

1 *philanthropist:* person who gives away money to help other people
2 *fortune:* a very large quantity of money
3 *disgrace:* something that brings shame or dishonor
4 In today's dollars, this is equivalent to approximately $8 billion.

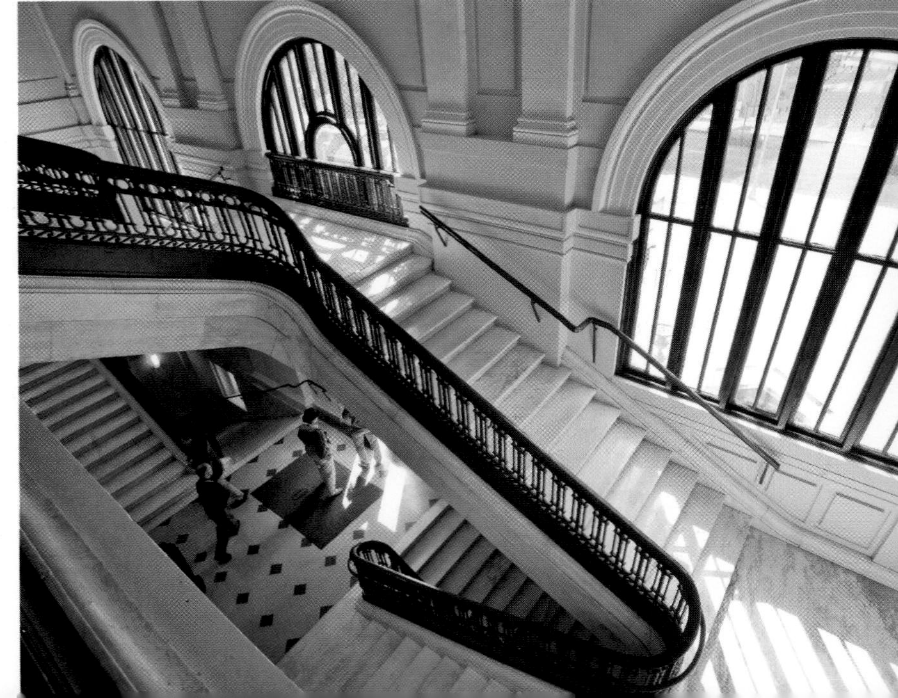

Elegant staircase inside the Carnegie Library building at Mt. Vernon Square, Washington, DC

COMPREHENSION CHECK Based on the reading, tell if the statement is true (**T**) or false (**F**).

1. The Carnegie family left Scotland because they saw more economic possibilities in the United States.
2. When Carnegie was young, he had no help from anyone.
3. Carnegie encouraged rich people to help others.

8.1 Infinitives—Overview

An infinitive is *to* + the base form of the verb: *to go, to be, to see.*

Examples	Explanation
Carnegie wanted **to help** others.	An infinitive is used after certain verbs.
He wanted rich people **to give** away their money.	An infinitive can be used after the object of the sentence.
I'm happy **to help**.	An infinitive can follow certain adjectives.
It's important **to help** others.	An infinitive follows certain expressions that begin with *it*.
To help others makes a person feel good.	An infinitive can be the subject of a sentence.
Do you volunteer your time in order **to help** others?	An infinitive can be used to show purpose.
He's old enough **to help**. She's too young **to help**.	An infinitive is used after expressions with *too* and *enough*.

Language Notes:

1. In a sentence with two infinitives connected by ***and*** or ***or***, the second *to* is usually omitted.
   I want **to make** money ***and*** **help** others.
   You can choose **to volunteer** time ***or*** **donate** money.
2. Put *not* before an infinitive to make it negative.
   Carnegie decided **not to die** rich.
3. For a passive infinitive, we use *to be* + past participle.
   Everyone wants **to be given** an opportunity to succeed.

CD 2
TR 7

EXERCISE 1 Fill in the blanks with the words you hear.

About 25 years ago, Leslie Natzke, an ESL teacher from Chicago, went to Niger __to work__ (1.) as a Peace Corps[5] volunteer. She was surprised ____________ (2.) that so few girls finished high school. According to an organization, Save the Children, Niger is the worst place in the world to be a mother. Very poor parents often marry off their daughters at a very young age in order ____________ (3.) money from the husband's family. Natzke thought that these girls were too young ____________ (4.) married and needed ____________ (5.) their education first.

[5] *Peace Corps:* an agency of the U.S. government that provides skilled volunteers to assist economic development in underdeveloped countries

continued

When Natzke returned to the United States, she continued ____________________ about the girls in
6.
Niger. She wanted ____________________ more for them. In 2008, she started a program called Expanding
7.
Lives. This program brings teenage girls from Niger to Chicago for the summer. At first, Natzke just wanted them ____________________ their education and ____________________ high school. Then she decided
8. 9.
____________________ leadership training.
10.

As the program grew, Natzke wanted the girls ____________________ about finance so that they could
11.
start a business back home. But most of all, she wanted them ____________________ health education.
12.
It is important for Natzke ____________________ these girls become leaders. She wants them
13.
____________________ their new skills to other girls in Niger and help them expand their lives too.
14.

____________________ experience with Americans, Natzke has found volunteer families that give these
15.
girls a place to live during the summer.

8.2 Verbs Followed by an Infinitive

Examples	Explanation
Carnegie **didn't want to die** rich. Natzke **decided to help** girls from Niger. Everyone **deserves to have** an education.	Some verbs can be followed by an infinitive.

Language Notes:

1. The verbs below can be followed by an infinitive:

agree	deserve	learn	prefer*	try*
appear	expect	like*	prepare	want
attempt	forget	love*	pretend	wish
begin*	hate*	manage	promise	
choose	hope	need	refuse	
continue*	intend	offer	seem	
decide	know how	plan	start*	

2. The following modal phrases are also followed by an infinitive: *can afford, can't stand**, would like.*

* These verbs can also be followed by a gerund with little or no change in meaning. See Chart 8.14

EXERCISE 2 Fill in the blanks with the infinitive form of one of the verbs from the box. You may use the same verb more than once.

help	use	make	give	persuade
follow	give away	get	provide	

Bill Gates and Warren Buffet, two of the richest people in the world, know how ___to make___ (1.) money. They want ___________ (2.) the example of Andrew Carnegie; they have also chosen ___________ (3.) others. They signed a document called the Giving Pledge, where they promise ___________ (4.) more than half of their wealth during their lifetimes. They want ___________ (5.) their money to make life better for others.

Gates and Buffet have managed ___________ (6.) over 100 American billionaires to sign the Giving Pledge. Pierre Omidyar, of eBay, has promised ___________ (7.) at least half of his wealth to charity. Now Gates and Buffet are attempting ___________ (8.) billionaires in other countries to sign the Giving Pledge too. Gates wants ___________ (9.) all children with a good education and medical care.

EXERCISE 3 Fill in the blanks with an infinitive. Use the verbs from the box.

give	build	learn	educate	get
die	work✓	have	start	leave

1. Andrew Carnegie started ___to work___ when he was very young.
2. His parents chose ___________ Scotland.
3. They hoped ___________ a better life in the U.S.
4. Carnegie wanted ___________ free public libraries.
5. He didn't want ___________ rich.
6. Children in all countries deserve ___________ a good education.
7. Everyone wants ___________ a chance to succeed in life. *(passive)*
8. In some countries, poor children can't go to school. Children in all countries need ___________. *(passive)*
9. Girls in Niger want ___________ a better life.
10. They need ___________ about computers, health, and finance.

EXERCISE 4 About You Assume you are a billionaire. Fill in the blank with an infinitive phrase to tell how you would like to help others. Share your answers with a partner.

I would like ____

8.3 Object before Infinitive

Some verbs can be followed by an object + an infinitive.

Examples	Explanation
Carnegie wanted **poor people to have** the same opportunities as rich people.	The object can be a noun.
He encouraged **them to use** use libraries.	The object can be a pronoun.

Language Note:

The verbs below can be followed by a noun or object pronoun + an infinitive:

advise	convince	invite	remind	want
allow	encourage	need	teach*	would like
ask	expect	permit	tell	
beg	force	persuade	urge	

* After *teach, how* is sometimes used: My parents taught me *how to help* others.

EXERCISE 5 Fill in the blanks with an object pronoun and the infinitive of one of the verbs from the box.

sign	help	buy	use✓	become	think	go
take	volunteer	suffer	save	finish	do	teach

1. **A:** My brother likes to buy a lot of expensive "toys."

   B: You should encourage ___him to use___ his money in better ways.

2. **A:** How do Bill and Melinda Gates persuade billionaires to give away their money?

   B: They talk to them. They encourage ___________(a.) about helping others. They ask ___________(b.) the Giving Pledge.

3. **A:** Andrew Carnegie's mother was worried about her children. She didn't want ___________(a.). She talked to her husband about the possibilities of a better life.

   B: What did she want ___________(b.)?

   A: She wanted ___________(c.) the family to America.

4. **A:** My sister is a very generous person.

   B. Do you mean she gives her children a lot of things?

   A: No. She teaches ______________ (a.) others.

   B: That's nice to hear. Those words encourage ______________ (b.) my children to be generous, too.

5. **A:** My parents weren't rich but they always helped other people.

   B: How did they do that?

   A: They donated their time. They taught ______________ (a.) during my free time. So I tutor high school kids after school. I want ______________ (b.) their education.

6. **A:** My parents always gave me money when I was a child.

   B: Did you buy a lot of toys?

   A: No. They didn't allow ______________ (a.) a lot of things. They encouraged ______________ (b.) my money.

   B: Save for what?

   A: I saved my money for a charity project.

7. **A:** Why does Leslie Natzke bring African girls to Chicago every summer?

   B: She wants ______________ (a.) to college. She also wants ______________ (b.) leaders and teach other girls.

EXERCISE 6 Change the following imperative statements to statements with an object pronoun plus an infinitive.

1. A woman says to her husband, "Teach the children good values."

   She wants *him to teach the children good values.*

2. My parents always said to me, "Help others."

   They expected ______________

3. A mother says to her children, "Don't forget about other people."

   She wants ______________

4. The father said to his children, "Give to charity."

   He advised ______________

continued

5. Parents say to their children, “Be kind to others.”

They want ______________________________

6. I said to you, “Work hard.”

I would like ______________________________

7. My parents said to us, “Give money to people in need."

They encouraged ______________________________

8. A father says to his daughter, “Be generous.”

He wants ______________________________

9. My parents said to me, “Don’t be selfish.”

They encouraged ______________________________

10. Parents say to their children, “Be polite.”

They expect ______________________________

EXERCISE 7 About You Use the verbs given to tell what your family wanted from you when you were growing up. Share your answers with a partner.

1. expect

My parents expected me to be polite.

2. advise

____

3. permit

____

4. tell

____

5. expect

____

6. encourage

____

8.4 Causative Verbs

Some verbs are called *causative* verbs because one person causes, enables, or allows another to do something.

Examples	Explanation
Gates **has gotten** billionaires **to sign** the Giving Pledge. Carnegie **persuaded** wealthy people **to give** away their money. You **convinced** me **to help** others.	*Get*, *persuade*, and *convince* are followed by an object + infinitive. *Get*, in this case, means persuade.
Carnegie **helped** people **(to) get** an education. Leslie **helps** girls **(to) improve** their lives.	After *help* + object, either the infinitive or the base form can be used. The base form is more common.
When Carnegie was a child, he met a rich man who had a small library. This man **let** children **use** his library. This man **permitted** children **to use** his library. This man **allowed** children **to use** his library.	*Let, permit,* and *allow* have the same meaning.
No one can **make** you **give** to charity. Giving to charity **makes** me **feel** good.	*Make* is followed by an object + base form. *Make* can mean *force*. *Make* can mean *cause something to happen.*
Warren Buffet **had** his children **sign** the Giving Pledge. The teacher **had** us **write** a composition about charity.	*Have* means to give a job or task to someone. *Have*, in this case, is followed by an object + base form.

EXERCISE 8 Circle the correct verb form to complete each conversation.

1. **A:** Do you always give to charity?

   B: I know I should. But I don't always do it.

   A: Whenever I get a gift in the mail from a charity, I send a check. I think this is a good way to get people (*give*/*to give*)[a.].

   B: What kind of gifts do you receive in the mail?

   A: I often get address labels. Don't you?

   B: Yes, but that doesn't persuade me (*donate*/*to donate*)[b.] money. I just use the labels and throw away the donation envelope.

continued

2. **A:** I volunteered for the public TV station last month.

B: What did they have you (*do/to do*)?
a.

A: My job was to address envelopes. It was fun. I met other volunteers. And it made me (*feel/to feel*)
b.
good about watching the station.

3. **A:** I have a doctor's appointment on Friday, and my car doesn't work.

B: Let me (*drive/to drive*) you.
a.

A: I don't want to bother you.

B: It's not a bother. I love to volunteer my time.

4. **A:** When I was a child, my parents gave me money once a week.

B: Did they let you (*buy/to buy*) whatever you wanted?
a.

A: They allowed me (*use/to use*) half of the money. They had me (*save/to save*) the other half.
b. c.
They convinced me (*give/to give*) part of my savings to charity.
d.

EXERCISE 9 Fill in the blanks with the base form or the infinitive of the verb given.

There are many ways to help others. Some people donate money. I volunteer for my local public radio station. The radio station needs money from listeners. Several times a year, the station tries to persuade listeners ___to give___ (1. give) money to the station. Without their support, the radio station could not exist. The station managers have us ______________ (2. answer) the phones when people call to contribute. We let callers ______________ (3. tell) us about their favorite programs. To get people ______________ (4. contribute), the station offers some gifts. For example, for a $60 contribution, you can get a coffee mug. For a $100 contribution, you can get a book. Everyone can listen to public radio for free. No one makes you ______________ (5. pay) for it. But listeners should pay for this service, if they can. I'd like to convince my friends ______________ (6. volunteer) or ______________ (7. send) in money.

8.5 Adjective plus Infinitive

Examples	Explanation
Some people are **happy to help** others. It makes me **sad to see** so many poor people. I am **proud to be** a volunteer. We are **pleased to help**.	Certain adjectives can be followed by an infinitive. Many of these adjectives describe a person's emotional or mental state.

Language Note:

The following adjectives can be followed by an infinitive:

afraid	eager	pleased	sad
ashamed	glad	prepared	sorry
delighted	happy	proud	surprised
disappointed	lucky	ready	willing

EXERCISE 10 A college student has volunteered her time with an agency that delivers food to poor families. She is discussing her duties with the volunteer coordinator. Fill in the blanks with an appropriate infinitive. Answers may vary.

A: Are you willing ___*to donate*___ (1.) your time on the weekends?

B: Yes. I'm eager ______________ (2.) people who need my help. I'm ready ______________ (3.) whatever you need me to do.

A: You're going to deliver meals to people in this neighborhood who don't have enough food.

B: I'm surprised ______________ (4.) that some people don't have enough to eat. This seems like a middle-class neighborhood.

A: It is. But the economy is bad. Most people are lucky ______________ (5.) a job. But some people have lost their jobs. Often people are ashamed ______________ (6.) for help.

B: I can understand that. But don't worry. I'm willing ______________ (7.) anyone who needs my help.

A: Don't be afraid ______________ (8.) into a stranger's home. Someone will always go with you.

B: I'm happy ______________ (9.) food to people who need it.

A: I'm glad that you're going to work with us. Your parents must be proud ______________ (10.) such a generous daughter.

B: And I'm lucky ______________ (11.) such generous parents. They taught me about giving when I was very young.

EXERCISE 11 Fill in the blanks with an infinitive or a base form in this conversation between an uncle and his nephew. Answers may vary.

A: What do you plan _____to do_____ (1.) this summer?

B: I wanted __________ (2.) a summer job, but I couldn't find one. It's going to be boring. I'm ready __________ (3.), but no one wants __________ (4.) me. And my parents expect me __________ (5.) a job. My mom won't let me __________ (6.) home all day and watch TV or hang out with my friends at the swimming pool.

A: Are you trying __________ (7.) money for your college education?

B: Not really. I haven't even thought about saving for college yet. I want a job because I'm planning __________ (8.) a car.

A: You need __________ (9.) about college too. You're going to graduate next year.

B: I'm planning __________ (10.) to a community college, so it won't be so expensive. And my parents are willing __________ (11.) for my college tuition.

A: Have you thought about volunteering your time this summer?

B: Not really. I just want __________ (12.) money.

A: Don't just think about money. Try __________ (13.) about how you can help other people. You can help little kids __________ (14.) to read. Or you can help __________ (15.) the parks by picking up garbage.

B: I keep telling you. I just want __________ (16.) money. What will I get if I do those things? I won't get my car.

A: You'll get satisfaction. Helping others will make you __________ (17.) good. And you'll learn __________ (18.) responsible. After you finish community college and go to a four-year college, it will look good on your application if you say you volunteered. It will help you __________ (19.) into a good college.

B: Why are you trying so hard to get me __________ (20.) a volunteer?

A: I volunteered when I was your age, and I found that it was more valuable than money.

B: OK. I'll volunteer if you're willing __________ (21.) me the money for the car.

ONE STEP at a TIME

CD 2
TR 8

Read the following article. Pay special attention to the words in bold.

Joyce Koenig, an artist, believes that it's important **to help** others. She heard of a summer camp in Wisconsin called One Step at a Time, for children with cancer. Even though these kids are sick, it's important for them **to have** fun too. It costs money for these kids **to go** to camp, so Joyce decided **to see** what she could do to help. It's impossible for her **to donate** a lot of money, so she had to think of another way **to help**.

She wanted **to combine** her love of art and her desire **to help** others. She had an idea: She started making and selling beautiful cards in order **to raise** money for these kids. Because these cards are all handmade, it was taking her a long time **to make** a lot of them. So Joyce had another idea. She started inviting friends to her house **to help** her make the cards. Often, she has card-making parties; the guests go into her studio and make the cards together. At first her friends were hesitant.[6] Many said that they were not artistic and didn't know how **to make** cards. But once they saw the beautiful materials that she had in her studio, her friends felt more comfortable designing, cutting, and pasting in order **to make** an original card.

But the materials are expensive. **To make** money without spending money, Joyce asks for and gets donations of paper, glue, scissors, ribbon, and other supplies from nearby stores. She sells her cards for $2 each at various art fairs during the year. Since she started her project, she has raised more than $40,000—two dollars at a time.

---

6 *hesitant:* unsure

COMPREHENSION CHECK Based on the reading, tell if the statement is true (**T**) or false (**F**).

1. Joyce uses her love of art to find a way to make money for kids with cancer.
2. To produce a large number of cards, she needed the help of her friends.
3. At first, her friends were eager to help her.

8.6 Infinitives as Subjects

Examples	Explanation
It's important **to help** other people. **It**'s fun **to make** cards. **It**'s possible **to get** materials for free.	An infinitive phrase can be the subject of a sentence. *It* introduces a delayed infinitive subject.
It is important **for Joyce to help** others. It wasn't possible **for her to make** a lot of cards by herself.	*For* + an object gives the infinitive a specific subject.
It costs a lot of money **to send** the kids to camp. **It takes** time and effort **to raise** money.	An infinitive is often used after *cost* + money and *take* + time.
It **took Joyce** three years to raise $30,000. It **costs her** very little to make cards.	An object can follow *take* and *cost*.
To give money away is the best thing rich people can do. **To help** others gives a person satisfaction.	Sometimes we begin a sentence with an infinitive phrase. A sentence that begins with an infinitive is formal.

EXERCISE 12 Fill in the blanks with any missing words.

1. It's enjoyable ___to___ make cards.
2. It doesn't __________ a lot of time to make a card.
3. __________ fun to get together and make cards.
4. It's not hard __________ Joyce's friends to make cards.
5. __________ help sick children is Joyce's goal.
6. It __________ only $2 __________ buy a card.
7. "__________ give away money is the best thing rich people can do," said Carnegie.

EXERCISE 13 Complete each statement with an infinitive phrase to talk about volunteering, donating money, etc. Share your answers with a partner.

1. It's important ___to think about the needs of others.___
2. It isn't necessary __________
3. It's a good idea __________
4. It's everyone's responsibility __________
5. It costs a lot of money __________
6. It's important __________
7. It takes a lot of time __________

8. It doesn't take long ______________________________

EXERCISE 14 Complete each statement. Begin with an *it* phrase. Share your answers with a partner.

1. It's impossible to get every billionaire to sign the Giving Pledge.
2. It isn't hard to get donations of materials.
3. ______________________ to help other people.
4. ______________________ to give away money.
5. ______________________ to die rich.
6. ______________________ to have a lot of money.
7. ______________________ not to have a good education.
8. ______________________ to live in the U.S.

EXERCISE 15 Change these statements to make them less formal by starting them with *it*.

1. To raise money for charity is a good thing.
   It's a good thing to raise money for charity.
2. To raise one million dollars is not easy.
   ____
3. To fight disease takes a lot of money.
   ____
4. To help poor people is everyone's responsibility.
   ____
5. To produce high-quality education takes a lot of money.
   ____
6. To build libraries was Carnegie's dream.
   ____
7. To raise money for sick children is Joyce's goal.
   ____
8. To fight disease in poor countries will take time.
   ____

8.7 Infinitives to Show Purpose

Examples	Explanation
Joyce sells cards **in order to raise** money.	*In order to* shows purpose. It answers the question *Why?* or *What for?*
Joyce sells cards **to raise** money.	*In order to* can be shortened. We can simply use *to*.
In order to raise money, Joyce sells cards.	The purpose phrase can come before the main clause. If so, we use a comma after the purpose phrase.

EXERCISE 16 Fill in the blanks to complete the sentences. Answers may vary.

1. In order to ___learn___ more about volunteering, you can use the Internet.
2. Carnegie donated his money to ________________ libraries.
3. You can volunteer in order to ________________ job experience.
4. To ________________ a job, you need experience. To ________________ experience, you need a job.
5. You can volunteer your time in order to ________________ people. There are many people who need help.
6. Joyce started making and selling cards in order to ________________ money to send kids to camp.
7. Leslie Natzke went to Africa in order ________________ in the Peace Corps.
8. She brings girls from Niger to Chicago ________________ them a better education.

8.8 Infinitives with *Too* and *Enough*

Examples	Explanation
This card is **too** big to fit in that envelope. I have **enough** time to make a card.	*Too* shows excess for a specific purpose. *Enough* shows sufficiency for a specific purpose.
You are never **too young to help** others. I worked **too slowly to finish** the card.	*too* + adjective/adverb + infinitive
I have **too much work to do**, so I have no time to volunteer. There are **too many problems** in the world **to solve** in one day.	*too much* + noncount noun + infinitive *too many* + plural count noun + infinitive
Am I **talented enough to design** a card? Joyce sells cards **easily enough to raise** money.	Adjective/adverb + *enough* + infinitive
I have **enough time to volunteer** this summer.	*enough* + noun + infinitive
Making cards is not too hard **for me to do**.	The infinitive phrase can be preceded by *for* + object.
I can't volunteer this summer because I'm **too busy**. Carnegie could build libraries because he had **enough money**.	Sometimes the infinitive phrase can be omitted. It is understood from the context: too busy = too busy to volunteer enough money = enough money to build libraries

EXERCISE 17 Fill in the blanks with the words given. Put the words in the correct order. Add *to* where necessary.

A: I heard about your card project, and I'd like to help you. But I don't have __enough talent__ (1. talent/enough).

I'm __________ (2. old/too/learn) something new.

B: It's so __________ (3. easy/make) cards. Anyone can do it.

A: I think it takes __________ (4. long/too/make) a card. I don't have __________ (5. time/enough)

and I'm not __________ (6. talented/enough).

B: It only takes about 15 minutes __________ (7. make) a card.

A: I'd really like to help but I'm __________ (8. busy/too/help) you at this time. I have

__________ (9. work/too much/do) at my job.

B: That's not a problem. When people have __________ (10. time/enough/help), they help. If not, that's okay too.

A: But I'd really like to help. Is there anything else I can do?

B: You can make a donation. You can buy just one card for $2.

A: Really? They're so inexpensive. I have __________ (11. money/enough/buy) five cards now.

B: Great! Every dollar helps.

EXERCISE 18 Fill in the blanks with *too, too much, too many,* or *enough* and any other words necessary to complete the conversation. Answers may vary.

A: I heard about a volunteer project at the park. Some friends and I are going to pick up garbage.

B: Why would you want to do that? I don't have __enough time__ (1.) to pick up garbage. I have

__________ (2.) things to do.

A: You always say you want to volunteer. About 50 volunteers are coming. It won't take

__________ (3.) to finish the job.

B: But it's __________ (4.) to spend the whole day in the sun. It's almost 90 degrees today.

A: We can go swimming afterwards. The park has a big swimming pool. You swim, right?

B: Yes, but I don't swim __________ (5.) to swim in deep water.

A: Don't worry. There's a shallow end and a deep end. You can stay in the shallow end.

B: The shallow end has a lot of kids. And the kids make __________ (6.) noise.

A: I guess you're just not interested in helping out.

HELPING OTHERS Get an EDUCATION

Matel Dawson

CD 2 TR 9

Read the following article. Pay special attention to the words in bold.

When we think of philanthropists, we usually think of the very rich and famous, like Andrew Carnegie or Bill Gates. However, Matel Dawson, a forklift[7] driver in Michigan, was an ordinary man who did extraordinary things.

Dawson started **working** at Ford Motor Company in 1940 for $1.15 an hour. By **working** hard, **saving** carefully, and **investing** his money wisely, he became rich. But he didn't care about **owning** expensive cars or **taking** fancy vacations. Instead of **spending** his money on himself, he enjoyed **giving** it away. During his lifetime, he donated more than $1 million for college scholarships to help students get an education.

Why did Dawson insist on **giving** his money away to students? One reason was that he did not have the opportunity to finish school. He had to drop out of school after the seventh grade to help support his poor family. He knew that not **having** an education limits job possibilities. Also, he learned about **giving** from his parents. He watched them work hard, save their money, and help others less fortunate. His mother made Dawson promise to always give something back. He was grateful to his parents for **teaching** him the importance of **helping** others.

When he became rich, he didn't change his lifestyle. He continued **driving** his old car and **living** in a one-bedroom apartment. And he didn't stop **working** until shortly before he died at the age of 81. When asked why he worked long past the time when most people retire, he replied, "It keeps me **going**, **knowing** I'm helping somebody."

[7] *forklift:* a vehicle used to lift and carry boxes

COMPREHENSION CHECK Based on the reading, tell if the statement is true (**T**) or false (**F**).

1. Matel Dawson started out poor but became rich.
2. When he was rich, he changed his lifestyle.
3. His goal was to help students get an education.

8.9 Gerunds—Overview

To form a gerund, we put an *-ing* ending on a verb. A gerund is used as a noun (subject or object).

Examples	Explanation
Contributing money is one way to help. **Volunteering** your time is another way to help.	A gerund (phrase) can be used as the subject.
Dawson started **working** in 1940. He continued **driving** an old car even after he became rich.	A gerund (phrase) can be used after the verb as the object.
Dawson insisted ***on*** **giving** away his money. He understood the importance ***of*** **helping** others.	A gerund (phrase) can be used as the object of a preposition.

Language Notes:

1. To make a gerund negative, we put *not* before the gerund.
   Not finishing high school limits job possibilities.
2. For a passive gerund, we use *being* + past participle.
   We appreciate **being given** the opportunity to have an education.
3. A gerund subject takes a singular verb.
   Helping others **gives** a person pleasure.

CD 2 TR 10

EXERCISE 19 Listen to the following article and fill in the blanks with the missing words.

Patty Stonesifer isn't worried about ___making___ (1.) money or __________ (2.) her career. She quit __________ (3.) for money and has started __________ (4.). She now works at Martha's Table, a Washington, DC, organization that is dedicated to __________ (5.) food, clothing, and education to poor people. What did Patty do before this? She made a lot of money __________ (6.) at Microsoft. In fact, she was the highest-ranking woman there. She helped start the Bill and Melinda Gates Foundation, which works on __________ (7.) preventable diseases in poor countries. But she didn't feel satisfied __________ (8.) so far away from the people she helped. She became more interested in __________ (9.) close to people who are in need. When she started her new volunteer job at Martha's Table, she tried __________ (10.) for a week on a food-stamp budget. She realized that __________ (11.) a healthy diet is impossible for low-income people. She's concerned about __________ (12.) healthy meals for as many hungry people as possible in DC, but mostly she's interested in __________ (13.) child hunger. She doesn't mind __________ (14.) long hours at Martha's Table without pay. And she doesn't miss __________ (15.) a fancy office. __________ (16.) something to help others gives her satisfaction.

8.10 Gerunds as Subjects

Examples	Explanation
Volunteering is enjoyable for Stonesifer. **Helping others** makes Stonesifer feel good.	A gerund or a gerund phrase can be the subject of the sentence.

EXERCISE 20 Fill in the blanks with a gerund. Answers may vary.

1. ___Giving___ away money made Dawson feel good.
2. ______ in a factory is not easy.
3. Not ______ an education always bothered Dawson.
4. ______ a college education is expensive in the U.S.
5. ______ money didn't give Dawson satisfaction.
6. ______ an old car was not a problem for Dawson.
7. ______ a vacation wasn't important for Dawson.
8. ______ that he was helping people was very important for Dawson.
9. ______ at Martha's Table gives Patty Stonesifer satisfaction.
10. ______ childhood hunger is Stonesifer's goal.

EXERCISE 21 Complete each statement. Answers will vary. Share your answers with a partner.

1. Owning a lot of things ___doesn't give people much satisfaction.___
2. Helping less fortunate people ______
3. Volunteering your time ______
4. Getting an education ______
5. Working hard ______

8.11 Gerunds after Prepositions and Nouns

Examples	Explanation
Dawson **didn't care about owning** fancy things. He **believed in helping** others.	Verb + preposition + gerund
Carnegie was **famous for building** libraries. Stonesifer is **concerned about helping** people.	Adjective + preposition + gerund
Dawson **thanked his parents for teaching** him to save money.	Verb + object + preposition + gerund
Dawson didn't **spend money going** on vacations or **eating** in expensive restaurants. Stonesifer **has satisfaction helping** others.	A gerund is used after the noun in the following expressions: *have a difficult time, have difficulty, have experience, have fun, have a good time, have a hard time, have a problem, have trouble, have satisfaction, spend time, spend money.*

EXERCISE 22 In the article from Exercise 19, some gerunds are preceded by a preposition. Circle the prepositions that precede a gerund.

EXERCISE 23 Fill in the blanks with a gerund from the box.

helping	quitting	creating	having
volunteering	giving	signing	providing
driving✓	building	making	selling

1. Dawson didn't have a problem ___driving___ an old car.
2. Dawson was interested in __________ students get an education.
3. He insisted on __________ away his money.
4. Stonesifer cares about __________.
5. She had a good reason for __________ her high-paying job.
6. She doesn't complain about not __________ a fancy office.
7. Carnegie was famous for __________ libraries.
8. Bill Gates is well-known for __________ Microsoft.
9. He's also well-known for __________ the Giving Pledge.
10. Joyce Koenig spends a lot of time __________ and __________ cards to help kids with cancer.
11. Leslie Natzke cares about __________ girls from Niger with a good education.

8.12 Prepositions after Verbs, Adjectives, and Nouns

Preposition Combinations		Common Phrases	Examples
Verb + Preposition	verb + *about*	care about complain about dream about forget about talk about think about worry about	You **care about helping** people.
	verb + *to*	adjust to look forward to object to	I **look forward to getting** a volunteer job.
	verb + *on*	depend on insist on plan on	Dawson **insisted on giving** away his money.
	verb + *in*	believe in succeed in	Bill Gates **succeeded in becoming** a billionaire.
Verb + Object + Preposition	verb + object + *of*	accuse . . . of suspect . . . of	You can't **accuse Gates of not caring** about other people.
	verb + object + *for*	apologize to . . . for blame . . . for forgive . . . for thank . . . for	Stonesifer **thanks her parents for teaching** her about charity.
	verb + object + *from*	keep . . . from prevent . . . from prohibit . . . from stop . . . from	No one could **stop Dawson from giving** away his money.
	verb + object + *about*	warn . . . about	Martha's Table **warns people about eating** too much junk food.

Adjective + Preposition	adjective + *of*	afraid of capable of guilty of proud of tired of	Dawson was **proud of helping** others get an education.
	adjective + *about*	concerned about excited about upset about worried about	Stonesifer was **excited about volunteering** with Martha's Table.
	adjective + *for*	responsible for famous for	Carnegie is **famous for building** public libraries.
	adjective + *to* + object + *for*	grateful to . . . for	He was **grateful to his parents for teaching** him about giving.
	adjective + *at*	good at successful at	Joyce is very **good at making** cards.
	adjective + *to*	accustomed to used to	Stonesifer is **accustomed to working** with poor people.
	adjective + *in*	interested in	Are you **interested in getting** a volunteer job?
Noun + Preposition	noun + *of*	in danger of in favor of the purpose of	My friends are **in favor of volunteering** on Saturday.
	noun + *for*	need for reason for excuse for technique for	What is Stonesifer's **reason for leaving** a high-paying job?

Language Notes:

1. *Plan, afraid,* and *proud* can be followed by an infinitive too.

   I **plan on volunteering** on weekends. / I **plan to volunteer** on weekends.

   I'm **afraid of making** a mistake. / I'm **afraid to make** a mistake.

   He's **proud of being** a volunteer. / He's **proud to be** a volunteer.

2. Sometimes *to* is part of an infinitive.

   I need ***to help*** my family.

3. Sometimes *to* is a part of a verb phrase and is followed by a gerund.

   I **look forward *to starting*** my new volunteer job.

EXERCISE 24 Fill in the blanks with a preposition and the gerund of the verb given. In some cases, no preposition is necessary.

A: My father's going to retire next month. He's worried ___about having___ (1. have) too much time on his hands.

B: I don't blame him ____________ (2. be) worried. For a lot of people, their self-worth depends ____________ (3. work), and when they retire, they feel empty.

A: My mother is afraid that he'll spend all his time ____________ (4. watch) TV. Besides, she's not accustomed ____________ (5. have) him home all day.

B: Doesn't he have any interests?

A: Well, he's interested ____________ (6. garden), but he lives in an apartment now, so he doesn't have a garden. When he had a house, he was always proud ____________ (7. have) the nicest garden on the block.

B: Has he thought ____________ (8. volunteer) at the Botanical Gardens?

A: Do they use volunteers?

B: I think so. He would have a great time ____________ (9. work) there.

A: You're right. He would be good ____________ (10. give) tours because he knows so much about flowers. Thank you ____________ (11. give) me this idea. I can't wait to tell him.

EXERCISE 25 About You Answer the questions. Discuss your answers with a partner.

1. Are you interested in helping other people? How?
2. In your native country, do some people have a hard time feeding their families? Is there help from the government or other organizations?
3. In your native country, is there someone who is famous for helping people in need?
4. Do you plan on volunteering in the future? If so, what kind of volunteer work interests you?

8.13 Verbs Followed by Gerunds

Examples	Explanation
Dawson enjoyed **giving** money away. He couldn't imagine not **helping** others. Students appreciate **receiving** financial aid.	Many verbs are followed by a gerund phrase.
My friend likes to **go bowling** on Saturdays, but I prefer volunteering.	*Go* + gerund is used in many idiomatic expressions of sports and recreation.

Here are expressions with *go* + gerund.

go boating	go fishing	go sailing	go skiing
go bowling	go hiking	go shopping	go swimming
go camping	go hunting	go sightseeing	
go dancing	go jogging	go skating	

Language Notes:

The following verbs can be followed by a gerund:

admit	can't stand[9]	dislike	keep (on)	postpone	resent
advise	consider	enjoy	like	practice	risk
appreciate	continue	finish	love	prefer	start
avoid	delay	follow	mind[10]	put off[11]	stop
begin	deny	hate	miss	quit	suggest
can't help[8]	discuss	imagine	permit	recommend	try

[8] *Can't help* means to have no control: When I see hungry children, I *can't help* feeling bad.
[9] *Can't stand* means can't tolerate: I *can't stand* seeing children go hungry.
[10] I *mind* means that something bothers me. I *don't mind* means that something is OK with me; it doesn't bother me.
[11] *Put off* means postpone: Don't *put off* applying for a volunteer position.

EXERCISE 26 Fill in the blanks with a gerund to complete these statements. Answers may vary.

1. Matel Dawson liked ___helping___ students.
2. Students appreciated __________________ help from Dawson.
3. He didn't mind __________________ an old car.
4. He didn't mind __________________ in a small apartment.
5. He kept on __________________ until shortly before he died at the age of 81.
6. People appreciate __________________ help from Stonesifer.
7. Stonesifer enjoys __________________ people with food, clothing, and an education.
8. At the end of the day, when she finishes __________________, she feels satisfied.

continued

9. She doesn't mind not __________________ money.

10. Joyce Koenig appreciates __________________ donated materials for her cards.

11. When she finishes __________________ cards, she tries to sell them at art fairs.

12. Leslie Natzke has many fun activities for her girls from Niger. It's hot in Chicago in the summer.

Sometimes they go __________________ in Lake Michigan.

8.14 Verbs Followed by a Gerund or Infinitive

Examples	Explanation
(a) Dawson liked **giving** money away. (b) He liked **to give** money away. (a) He started **working** in 1940. (b) He started **to work** in 1940.	Some verbs can be followed by either a gerund (a) or an infinitive (b) with no difference in meaning.

Language Note:

The verbs below can be followed by either a gerund or an infinitive with no difference in meaning:

begin continue like prefer hate love start can't stand

EXERCISE 27 In the following sentences, change gerunds to infinitives and infinitives to gerunds.

1. Dawson's parents loved to help others.

   Dawson's parents loved helping others.

2. They hated seeing people suffer.

   They hated to see people suffer.

3. Dawson began working when he was 19 years old.

   ____

4. He liked giving away money.

   ____

5. He continued to work until he was 80 years old.

   ____

6. He preferred to live in a small apartment.

   ____

7. He loved to help students get an education.

   ____

EXERCISE 28 This is a conversation between a teenager and her older brother. Fill in the blanks with an appropriate gerund or infinitive. It doesn't matter which one you use. Answers may vary.

A: I want to work this summer, but I can't decide what to do.

B: How about volunteering in a museum?

A: I can't stand being OR to be (1.) indoors all day. I prefer ________ (2.) outdoors.

B: You're a great swimmer. Why don't you volunteer to teach kids how to swim?

A: I hate ________ (3.) with kids. It's hard work.

B: Well, what do you like?

A: I love ________ (4.) at the beach.

B: Maybe you should get a job as a lifeguard.

A: Great idea! I'll start ________ (5.) for a job tomorrow.

B: That's what you said yesterday.

A: I guess I'm lazy. I just don't like ________ (6.).

8.15 Gerund or Infinitive as Subject

Either a gerund or an infinitive can be the subject of the sentence with no difference in meaning.

Examples	Explanation
Helping others makes me feel good.	A gerund phrase can be used as the subject.
It makes me feel good **to help others**.	An infinitive phrase can be a delayed subject.
To help others makes me feel good.	An infinitive phrase can begin a sentence.

EXERCISE 29 Change these statements to begin with a gerund phrase.

1. It is wonderful to help others.

   Helping others is wonderful.

2. It costs a lot of money to go to college.

   ____

3. It is hard to work and study at the same time.

   ____

continued

4. It is important to help students get an education.

____

5. It is difficult to work in a factory.

____

6. To die rich is a disgrace (according to Carnegie).

____

7. It is satisfying to help others.

____

8. It is a wonderful thing to sign the Giving Pledge.

____

8.16 Gerund or Infinitive after a Verb: Differences in Meaning

Examples	Explanation
Dawson loved to work. He didn't **stop working** until he was 80.	*Stop* + gerund = quit or discontinue an activity
Dawson wanted to finish school, but he **stopped to get** a job.	*Stop* + infinitive = quit one activity in order to start another activity
Do you **remember reading** about Carnegie?	*Remember* + gerund = remember that something happened earlier
Dawson's mother said, "Always **remember to help** other people."	*Remember* + infinitive = remember something and then do it
I **tried working** with kids but didn't like it. Then I **tried volunteering** at the park.	*Try* + gerund = experiment with something new. You try one method, and if that doesn't work, you try a different method.
Joyce **tries to sell** her cards at art fairs. She **tries to make** money for sick kids.	*Try* + infinitive = make an effort or an attempt

Language Note:
There is a big difference between *stop/remember* + gerund and *stop/remember* + infinitive. For *try*, the difference is mostly evident in the past tense.

EXERCISE 30 Read the following conversation between a son and his mother. Fill in the blanks with the gerund or infinitive of the word given.

A: Hi, Mom. I'm calling to say good-bye. I'm leaving for California tomorrow.

B: Really? You didn't tell me about it.

A: Of course I did. I remember ___telling___ (1. tell) you about it when I was at your house for dinner last week.

B: Oh, yes. Now I remember ____________________ you say something about it. Why are you going?
2. hear

A: I have a friend there, and we've decided to do some volunteer work in a forest this summer.

B: Have I met your friend?

A: He was at my birthday party last year. You met him then.

B: I don't remember ____________________ him. Anyway, how are you getting to California?
3. meet

A: I'm driving.

B: Alone?

A: Yes.

B: If you get tired, you should stop ____________________ at a rest area. And you can stop
4. rest

____________________ a cup of coffee every few hours.
5. get

A: I will.

B: Don't stop ____________________ strangers. It could be dangerous.
6. pick up

A: Of course I won't.

B: And remember ____________________ your cell phone on in case I want to call you. Last night I wanted
7. leave

to talk to you, and I couldn't reach you. First I tried ____________________ your cell phone. Then I tried
8. call

____________________ your home phone. But all I got was your voice mail.
9. call

A: Did you leave a message?

B: I tried ____________________ a message but your mailbox was full. Then I tried ____________________
10. leave 11. text

you. But you didn't answer.

A: Don't worry. I'll leave my phone on.

B: You'll be outdoors all day for your job. Remember ____________________ sunscreen. You don't want to get
12. use

sunburn.

A: Mom, stop ____________________ so much. And stop ____________________ me so much advice. I'm
13. worry 14. give

twenty-four years old!

B: Try ____________________. I'm your mother. Of course I worry.
15. understand

Dan Pallotta

AIDS BIKE RIDES

Read the following article. Pay special attention to the words in bold.

In 1994, a Californian named Dan Pallotta **saw** many people around him **die** of AIDS. He wanted to see what he could do to raise money for AIDS research. He organized a bike ride from Los Angeles to San Francisco. Each rider asked friends and relatives to give donations to support the ride. His AIDS rides continued to grow. In nine years, 182,000 riders participated, raising almost six hundred million dollars for AIDS research. Many more organizations started to have AIDS bike rides, raising millions of dollars.

Mimi Gordon, who has done several AIDS rides, wrote in her journal:

Before I went on my first AIDS ride, I **used to think** that one person's contribution is not very important. But I was wrong. In 1998, I went on my first AIDS ride, from San Francisco to Los Angeles. Even though I bike to and from work every day (twenty miles round trip), I **wasn't used to riding** long distances. Also, I live in Chicago, where the land is flat, so I **wasn't used to riding** in hills and mountains. I trained for about six months before the ride, riding at least 150 miles a week.

I **used to own** a ten-speed road bike, but I realized that I would need something better for the long, hilly ride. I bought a new twenty-four-speed mountain bike. I completed the ride and raised almost five thousand dollars for AIDS research. I felt so good about it that I started looking for more rides to do.

In 2001, I did the Alaska ride, which was especially difficult. It was mountainous, but that was not all: It was much colder than expected. Some of the riders couldn't **get used to** the cold and had to quit. But I'm proud to say that I finished it and went on to do four more AIDS rides.

COMPREHENSION CHECK Based on the reading, tell if the statement is true (**T**) or false (**F**).

1. In the first year of the AIDS ride, Dan Pallotta raised $600 million.
2. The first AIDS ride was from Los Angeles to San Francisco.
3. Mimi did a total of four AIDS rides.

8.17 *Used To / Be Used To / Get Used To*

Examples	Explanation
Mimi **used to own** a 10-speed bike. Now she owns a 24-speed bike. I didn't **use to exercise much**. Now I exercise almost every day.	*Used to* + the base form shows that an activity was repeated or habitual in the past. This activity has been discontinued. For the negative, we use *didn't use to.* We omit the *d* in the negative.
Mimi **is used to riding** her bike in Chicago, which is flat. She **isn't used to the cold wind** in Alaska.	*Be used* to + gerund or noun means to be accustomed to. This phrase describes a person's habits. It shows what is normal and comfortable. For the negative, we use *be* + *not* + *used to.* We don't omit the *d* in the negative.
Chicago is flat. Mimi had to **get used to** riding her bike in the mountains. Some of the riders **couldn't get used to** the cold wind and had to quit.	*Get used to* + gerund or noun means "become accustomed to." For the negative, we often use *can't* or *couldn't* before *get used to.* We don't omit the *d* in the negative.

Pronunciation Note:
The *d* in *used to* is not pronounced.

EXERCISE 31 Finish these statements. Answers may vary.

1. I used to ___exercise once a week___, but now I exercise every day.
2. I used to ______________ to work. Now I ride my bike. It's good exercise and I save money.
3. I used to ______________ that one person can't make a difference. Now I know that everyone can make a difference.
4. I used to ______________ my bike only in the summer. But now I do it all year round.
5. I used to ______________ only money. Now I donate time and money to help others.
6. I used to ______________ my extra money, but now I donate it to charity.

EXERCISE 32 Fill in the blanks with *be used to* and the correct form of the verb given.

1. **A:** I heard you volunteer with children now. Do you like it?

   B: I'm not sure yet. I've always worked with adults. I___'m not used to working___ (work) with children.

2. **A:** Do you want to train for the next California AIDS ride with me?

   B: California is mountainous. I ______________ (ride) a bike in the mountains, so I think it's going to be hard for me.

continued

3. **A:** Do you think it's hard for Bill Gates to give away money?

B: I don't think so. He's been doing it for a long time. So I think he ______________ (give) away a lot of money.

4. **A:** Don't you think the story about Dawson is strange?

B: Why?

A: He had a lot of money but he continued to drive his old car.

B: Well, he ______________ (drive) his old car. So it wasn't a problem for him.

5. **A:** Patty Stonesifer had a high-paying job, but now she works with people in need. It must be hard.

B: She loves it. She learned from her parents to help others. So she ______________ (help) other people.

6. **A:** I have a volunteer job on the weekends.

B: Do you like it?

A: I like the job, but I ______________ (work) on the weekend. I always used to relax and watch sports on TV on the weekend.

7. **A:** Joyce invites people to her house to make cards.

B: I'm glad she's not inviting me. I ______________ (**a.** do) anything artistic.

A: Everyone tells her the same thing. She ______________ (**b.** hear) that. But she always explains that no artistic talent is necessary.

8. **A:** I want to do an AIDS bike ride. I have a lot of experience riding a bike.

B: Why don't you do it, then?

A: There's just one problem. I'm from Thailand, where we always ride on the left side of the street. I ______________ (ride) on the right side. I'm afraid I'll have an accident.

EXERCISE 33 Here is a story of a San Francisco man who did the Alaska AIDS ride. Circle the correct words to complete the story.

In 2001, I went on the AIDS bike ride in Alaska. My friends told me about it and asked me to join them. At first I was afraid. My friends are good bikers. They (*used to ride/are used to riding*) 1. long distances because they do it all the time. They persuaded me to try it because it was for such a good cause. To get ready for the ride, I had to make some lifestyle changes. (*I'm/I*) 2. used to be a little overweight, so I had to slim down and get in shape. First, I went on a diet. (*I/I was*) 3. used to eating a lot of meat, but now I eat mostly vegetables and fish. Also, I decided to get more exercise. I used to (*take/taking*) 4. the bus to work every day, but I decided to start riding my bike to work. I work ten miles from home, so it was hard for me at first. But little by little, I (*got used to/used to*) 5. it. On the weekends, I started to take longer rides. Eventually I got used to (*ride/riding*) 6. about 45–50 miles a day. When the time came for the AIDS ride, I thought I was prepared. I live in San Francisco, which is hilly, so I was used to (*ride/riding*) 7. up and down hills. But it's not cold in San Francisco. On some days the temperature in Alaska was only 25 degrees Fahrenheit, with strong winds. At first I (*wasn't/couldn't*) 8. get used to the cold. It was especially hard to (*used/get used*) 9. to the strong winds. But eventually, I got (*use/used*) 10. to it. I am proud to say I was one of the 1,600 riders who finished the ride. I didn't (*use/used*) 11. to think that one person could make a difference, but I raised close to $4,000. As a group we raised $4 million. And I've become a much healthier person because of this experience.

Cyclists during an AIDS Day Bike Ride in Davis, California

8.18 Sense-Perception Verbs

After sense-perception verbs, we can use either the *-ing* form or the base form with only a slight difference in meaning.

Examples	Explanation
I **heard** you **talk** about the Giving Pledge a few days ago. Dan Pallotta **saw** many people around him **die** of AIDS.	When the base form is used after a sense-perception verb (*saw, heard,* etc.), it indicates completion.
I **heard** you **talking** about a charity project. I **saw** some teenagers **volunteering** in the park last week.	When the *-ing* form is used after a sense-perception verb, it shows that something is sensed while it is in progress. I heard you **while you were talking** about a charity project. I saw teenagers **who were volunteering** in the park.

Language Note:

The sense-perception verbs are: *hear, listen, feel, smell, see, watch, observe.*

EXERCISE 34 Fill in the blanks with the base form or *-ing* form of the verb given. In some cases, both forms are possible.

By their example, my parents always taught me to help others. One time, when I was a child on the way to a birthday party with my father, we saw a small boy ___walking___ (1. walk) alone on the street. As we approached him, we heard him __________ (2. cry). My father went up to him and asked him what was wrong. The boy said that he was lost. I saw my father __________ (3. take) his hand and heard him __________ (4. tell) the boy that he would help him find his parents. My father called the police. Even though we were in a hurry to go to the party, my father insisted on staying with the boy until the police arrived. I really wanted to go to the party and started to cry. I felt my father __________ (5. take) my hand and talk to me softly. He said, "We can't enjoy the party while this little boy is alone and helpless." Before the police arrived, I saw a woman __________ (6. run) in our direction. It was the boy's mother. She was so grateful to my father for helping her son that she offered to give him money. I heard my father __________ (7. tell) her, "I can't take money from you. I'm happy to be of help to your son."

I hear so many children today __________ (8. say), "I want" or "Buy me" or "Give me." I think it's important to teach children to think of others before they think of themselves. If they see their parents __________ (9. help) others, they will probably grow up to be charitable people.

SUMMARY OF LESSON 8

Infinitives and Base Forms

Examples	Explanation
Matel Dawson *wanted* **to help** others.	An infinitive is used after certain verbs.
His mother wanted *him* **to help** others.	An infinitive can follow an object noun or pronoun.
He was *happy* **to give** away his money.	An infinitive can follow certain adjectives.
We sell cards (**in order**) **to raise** money.	An infinitive is used to show purpose.
It's important **to help** others. **To help** others is our moral obligation.	INFORMAL: *It* introduces a delayed infinitive subject. FORMAL: The infinitive can be in the subject position.
It's good *for people* **to help** others. It's fun *for me* **to volunteer**.	*For* + noun or object pronoun is used to give the infinitive a subject.
I have *enough* time **to volunteer**. Dawson was *too* poor **to finish** school.	An infinitive can be used after a phrase with *too* and *enough*.
He often *heard* his mother **talk** about helping.	After sense perception verbs, a base form is used for a completed action.
It is important **to be loved**.	An infinitive can be used in the passive voice.
She *let* me **work**. She *made* me **work**. She *had* me **work**. She *got* me **to work**. She *convinced* me **to work**. She *persuaded* me **to work**.	After causative verbs *let, make*, and *have*, we use the base form. After causative verbs *get, convince*, and *persuade*, we use the infinitive.
He *helped* students **to get** an education. He *helped* them **pay** their tuition.	After *help*, either the infinitive or the base form can be used.

Gerunds

Examples	Explanation
Going to college is expensive in the U.S.	A gerund can be the subject of the sentence.
Dawson *enjoyed* **giving** money away.	A gerund follows certain verbs.
He learned *about* **giving** from his parents.	A gerund can be used after a preposition.
He had a hard *time* **supporting** his family.	A gerund is used after certain nouns.
Those teenagers over there are volunteers. You can *see* them **cleaning** the park.	An *-ing* form is used after sense perception verbs to describe an action in progress.
He doesn't like to **go shopping**.	A gerund is used in many expressions with *go*.
I appreciate **being given** an education.	A gerund can be used in the passive voice.

Gerund or Infinitive—Differences in Meaning

Examples	Explanation
I **used to spend** all my extra money. Now I save it.	Discontinued past habit
Patty **is used to working** in a poor neighborhood.	Present custom
Mimi always rode her bike on flat land. It was hard for her to **get used to riding** in the mountains.	Change of custom
Bicyclists can **stop to rest** when they get tired.	Stop one activity in order to do something else
When I was younger, I did the AIDS ride. I **stopped doing** it because it's too hard for me now.	Stop something completely
I **try to give** a little money to charity each year.	Make an attempt or effort
My old bike wasn't good enough for the ride. I **tried using** a mountain bike, and it was much better.	Experiment with a different method
Remember to help other people.	Remember and then do
Do you **remember reading** about Patty Stonesifer?	Remember something about the past

TEST/REVIEW

Fill in the blanks with the correct form of the verb given. Add prepositions, if necessary. In some cases, more than one answer is possible.

It's difficult for a college student to have (1. have) time for anything else but studying. But when Charity Bell was a student at Harvard, she made time in her busy schedule ________ (2. help) babies in need.

When Bell was 23, she became interested ________ (3. help) needy babies. She was volunteering at a children's hospital. The volunteer organization wanted her ________ (4. read) to the kids and ________ (5. play) games with them. The parents of these very sick children were there too, but they were often too tired ________ (6. read) or ________ (7. play) with their kids. They were grateful to her ________ (8. help) them. One day she went to the hospital and heard a baby ________ (9. cry) loudly in the next room. She went into that room and picked up the baby; the baby immediately stopped ________ (10. cry). She stayed with the baby for a few hours. When she began ________ (11. leave), the baby started ________ (12. cry) again. Bell asked the nurse about this baby, and the nurse told her that the baby was taken away from her parents and they couldn't find a temporary home for her.

The next day, Bell started ________ (13. learn) about how to be a foster parent. She made herself available to help on nights and weekends. Her phone started ________ (14. ring) immediately. She got used to ________ (15. pick) up the phone in the middle of the night. She became accustomed ________ (16. take) in children all the time. Before she started taking care of babies, she used to ________ (17. sleep) seven or eight hours a night. Then she had to get used to ________ (18. sleep) only three or four hours a night.

By the time she was 28 years old and in graduate school, Bell had been a foster mother to 50 children. ________ (19. complete) her studies, she had to take "her" babies to class with her. Her professors let her ________ (20. do) this. They understood that it was necessary for her ________ (21. study) and ________ (22. take) care of the babies at the same time. And her classmates didn't complain about ________ (23. have) a baby in the back of the class. Everyone understood how important it was for her ________ (24. help) these babies.

Even though Bell is sometimes tired, she is never too tired ________ (25. take) in a child that needs her. She gets very little money for ________ (26. take) care of these children. However, she gets great satisfaction ________ (27. watch) a baby ________ (28. grow). ________ (29. see) her babies ________ (30. leave) is always a bit sad for her, but there are more babies who need her. ________ (31. bring) love to a child is her greatest joy.

WRITING

PART 1 Editing Advice

1. Don't forget *to* when introducing an infinitive.

   He wants ^to help other people.

   It's important ^to be a charitable person.

2. Don't omit *it* when introducing a delayed infinitive.

   ~~Is~~ It's important for rich people to help others.

3. After *want, need,* and *expect,* use the object pronoun, not the subject pronoun, before the infinitive.

   My parents want ~~that I~~ me to donate money to charity.

4. Don't use *to* between *cost* or *take* and the indirect object.

   It costs ~~to~~ Leslie five thousand dollars to bring a girl to the U.S. from Niger.

   It took ~~to~~ him twenty hours to finish the bike ride.

5. Use *for,* not *to,* when you give a subject to the infinitive.

   It is easy ~~to~~ for me to ride my bike on flat land.

6. Use *to* + base form, not *for,* to show purpose.

   Carnegie worked hard ~~for~~ to build libraries.

7. Use a gerund or an infinitive, not a base form, as a subject.

   Help^ing others makes me feel good. OR It makes me feel good to help others.

8. Don't confuse *used to* and *be used* to.

   I ~~am~~ used to drive to school. Now I ride my bike.

   I've lived in Alaska all my life and I love it. I^'m used to ~~live~~ living in Alaska.

9. Be careful to use the correct form after *stop.*

   The story about Dawson was so interesting. I can't stop ~~to~~ think^ing about it.

10. Use a gerund, not an infinitive, after a preposition.

    Have you ever thought about ~~to~~ volunteer^ing with children?

11. Make sure to choose a gerund after certain verbs and an infinitive after others.

    I enjoy ~~to~~ help^ing other people.

    He decided ~~volunteering~~ to volunteer in the public library.

12. Use a base form after a sense-perception verb that shows completion.

I saw Mimi ~~to~~ finish her bike ride.

13. Use the base form, not the infinitive, after causative verbs *let, make*, and *have*.

Bill Gates has billionaires ~~to~~ sign the Giving Pledge.

PART 2 Editing Practice

Some of the shaded words and phrases have mistakes. Find the mistakes and correct them. If the shaded words are correct, write *C*.

It's important for (1. C) everyone (to) do (2.) something for others. I often thought about to help (3.) other people. My parents wanted that I help (4.) in their business, but I saw my parents to work (5.) too hard, and they had very little satisfaction from it or time for our family. I decided become (6.) a nurse instead. It took to (7.) me three years to complete (8.) the nursing program, and I'm happy I did it. First, find (9.) a job was easy because nurses are always in demand. Second, I enjoy working (10.) with sick people and make (11.) them to feel (12.) better. Some of my friends think is (13.) depressing to work (14.) with sick people all day, but it's easy for (15.) me to do (16.) it because I love helping (17.) people.

There's one thing I don't like about my job: I have to work (18.) nights, from 11 p.m. to 7 a.m. At first, I couldn't get used to sleep (19.) in the day. My kids are home on Saturday and Sunday, and when I was trying sleeping (20.), they sometimes wouldn't stop to make (21.) noise. When they were younger, they're used to make (22.) a lot of noise, but now that they're older, they understand. My wife made them understand (23.) that their dad needed his sleep and she needed them be (24.) quiet in the morning. My daughter is now thinking about become (25.) a nurse too.

People work for (26.) make money, but it's important for (27.) everyone finding (28.) a job that they love. Working (29.) as a nurse has been wonderful for me. I get a lot of satisfaction helping (30.) other people.

PART 3 Write About It

1. Andrew Carnegie wrote: "It is not good to have money if your spirit is poor." Describe what it means to have a rich spirit or a poor spirit. Give examples using people you know or have read about.
2. How does volunteering enrich the life of the volunteer?

PART 4 Edit Your Writing

Reread the Summary of Lesson 8 and the editing advice. Edit your writing from Part 3.

LESSON

Adverbial Clauses and Phrases
Sentence Connectors (Conjunctive Adverbs)
So/Such That for Result

COMING TO AMERICA

The sun sets behind the Statue of Liberty, an American symbol of freedom.

Everywhere immigrants have enriched and strengthened the fabric of American life.

—John F. Kennedy

A NATION of IMMIGRANTS

CD 2 TR 12 Read the following article. Pay special attention to the words in bold.

Ever since the United States became a country, it has been a nation of immigrants. The United States takes in more foreigners than the rest of the world combined, almost one million a year.

It is not uncommon for Americans to ask each other about their family background. Except for Native Americans, Americans have their roots in one or more countries. **Even though they are proud to be Americans**, many people often use two or more words to describe their national identity: "I'm Greek American," or "I'm an African American," or "I'm one-fourth English, one-fourth Irish, and one-half Polish."

Why have so many people chosen to leave everything behind to come to a new land **in spite of the hardships**[1] **they face**? The answer to that question is as diverse as the people who have come to the United States. In the 1600s, the first group of immigrants were the Pilgrims, who left England **to seek** religious freedom in America. Many other groups followed **to escape** hardship or **to find** opportunity.

In the 1800s, Germans came **because of political unrest and economic problems in Germany**. Irish and Chinese people came **because of famine in their countries**. At the beginning of the twentieth century, many Jews came from Eastern Europe **in order to escape** religious persecution.[2] Many Italians came **for** work.

By 1910, almost 15 percent of the population was foreign born. Some people thought: **if immigration continues at this pace**, the United States will lose its "American" identity. In 1924, Congress passed a law limiting the number of immigrants. By 1970, less than 5 percent of the population was foreign born, an all-time low.

In 1965, Congress passed a bill allowing more immigrants to come, and the foreign-born population started to rise quickly. In the 1970s, Vietnamese and Cambodians came **because of war**. Immigration from Asian countries quadrupled. Many others, such as Bosnians and Iraqis, came **because their countries were at war**. And, as always, people came **so that they could be reunited with family members who had come before**.

According to the 2010 census, 12.9 percent of the population was foreign born, with most of the immigrants from Asia and Latin America. In addition to legal immigration, about 11.7 million immigrants are living in the United States illegally. **Since the U.S. Census cannot count these people**, this number is only an estimate.

The United States is and has always been perceived as the land of freedom and opportunity.

Foreign-Born Population and Percentage of Total Population, for the United States: 1850 to 2010

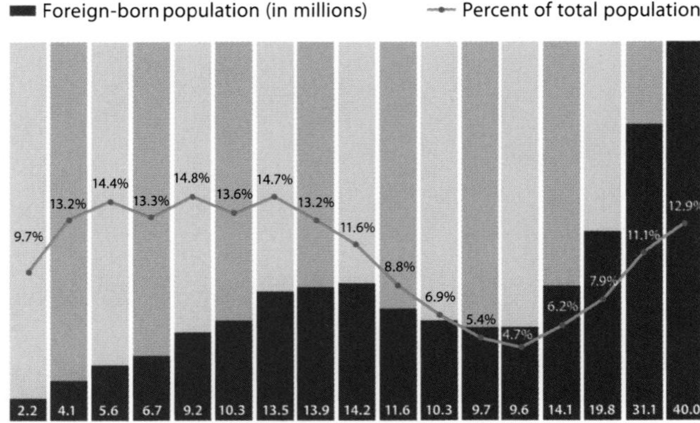

Source: U.S. Census Bureau, Census of Population, 1850 to 2000 and the American Community Survey, 2010.

---

[1] *hardship:* difficulty

[2] *persecution:* unjust or cruel treatment because of differences in belief

COMPREHENSION CHECK Based on the reading, tell if the statement is true (**T**) or false (**F**).

1. The highest percentage of foreign-born Americans was in 1910.
2. Americans often identify themselves with the nationality of their ancestors.
3. Most of the immigrants coming to America today are from Europe.

9.1 Adverbial Clauses and Phrases—Introduction

Some sentences have an adverbial clause or phrase and a main clause.

Examples	Explanation
Before the 1960s, more than half of immigrants came from Europe.	An adverbial clause or phrase can show **time**.
Germans came to the U.S. **because of economic problems in Germany**.	An adverbial clause or phrase can show **reason**.
Many immigrants come **so that they can be reunited with family members**.	An adverbial clause or phrase can show **purpose**.
Even though it's hard to be an immigrant, many people make that choice.	An adverbial clause or phrase can show **contrast**.
If there is a war in a country, many people leave that country.	An adverbial clause or phrase can show **condition**.

Language Note:

The adverbial clause or phrase can come before or after the main clause. If it comes before, it is usually separated from the main clause with a comma.

I went to Canada before I came to the United States. (NO COMMA)
Before I came to the United States, I went to Canada. (COMMA)

EXERCISE 1 Listen to the following story about the author's family. Fill in the blanks with the words you hear.

CD 2 TR 13

I'm a Jewish American. My maternal grandfather came to the United States from Poland in 1911 ___because___ (1.) he wanted a better life for his wife and children. Life was hard for them in Poland, and they had heard stories of how you could better yourself in America ___________ (2.) you were poor. ___________ (3.) my grandfather was working as a tailor in Chicago, he saved money ___________ (4.) he could bring his family to join him. ___________ (5.) ten years of hard work, he had finally saved up enough money. ___________ (6.) he had been in the United States for ten years, he didn't learn much English ___________ (7.) he had to go to work immediately.

continued

__________ (8.) my grandmother and her four children started their journey in 1921, they had never left their village before. They arrived in New York __________ (9.) that was the entry point for most immigrants at that time. They were tired and scared __________ (10.) they didn't speak one word of English. They were afraid of what to do next, __________ (11.) finally, they saw my grandfather waiting for them. The immigration officials detained them in New York __________ (12.) my mother's youngest sister was sick. At that time, you couldn't enter the country __________ (13.) your health was good. She was taken to a hospital. __________ (14.) she was in the hospital for one week, she was released and the family was ready to start their new life. From New York, they took a train to Chicago. __________ (15.) they arrived in Chicago, my mother, the oldest, was sixteen years old. She went to work in a factory __________ (16.) she could help her younger brother and sisters get an education.

EXERCISE 2 In Exercise 1, tell if the filled in words express time (T), reason (R), purpose (P), contrast (Ct), or condition (Cd).

1. R	5. ______	9. ______	13. ______
2. ______	6. ______	10. ______	14. ______
3. ______	7. ______	11. ______	15. ______
4. ______	8. ______	12. ______	16. ______

Immigrants arrive at Ellis Island in the early 1900s.

9.2 Reason and Purpose

Examples	Explanation
My family left Poland **because they wanted to improve their lives**.	*Because* introduces a clause of reason.
My grandfather didn't have time to go to school **because of his job**.	*Because of* introduces a noun or noun phrase.
Since the U.S. Census cannot count illegal immigrants, their number is only an estimate.	*Since* means *because*. It is used to introduce a fact. The main clause is the result of this fact.
The Pilgrims came **in order to seek religious freedom**. Vietnamese people came **to escape war**.	*In order to* shows purpose. The short form is *to*. We follow *to* with the base form of the verb.
My grandmother came **so that the family could be reunited**. He wants his wife to come next year **so they can be together again**.	*So that* shows purpose. The short form is *so*. The purpose clause usually contains a modal: *can, will,* or *may* for future; *could, would,* or *might* for past.
She came to the U.S. **for a better life**.	*For* shows purpose. *For* is followed by a noun (phrase).

Language Notes:

1. Remember: *Since* can also be used to show time. The context tells you the meaning of *since*.
   He has been in the U.S. **since** 2003. (time)
   Since my grandfather had to work hard, he didn't have time to study English. (reason)
2. *So* is also used to show result. The context tells you the meaning of *so*.
   I came to the U.S. alone, **so** I miss my family. (result)
   I came to the U.S. **so (that)** I could get an education. (purpose)
   Notice that a comma is used for result but not for purpose.

EXERCISE 3 Fill in the blanks with *because, because of, since, for, (in order) to,* or *so (that).*

1. Many immigrants came to the U.S. ___(in order) to___ escape famine.
2. Many immigrants came ____________ they didn't have enough to eat.
3. ____________ they could give their children a good education, many immigrants came to the U.S.
4. ____________ the political situation, many people left their countries.
5. Many immigrants came ____________ they could escape war.
6. Many immigrants came ____________ the poor economy in their countries.
7. Many immigrants came ____________ be reunited with their relatives.
8. ____________ war destroyed their homes, many people left their countries.
9. ____________ escape poverty, many immigrants came to the U.S.

continued

10. Often immigrants come ________________ they want a better future for their children.

11. Immigrants come to the U.S. ________________ a better life.

EXERCISE 4 Complete the conversation using *because, because of, for, since, so (that),* or *(in order) to.* Answers may vary.

A: I heard you moved.

B: Yes. We moved last month. We bought a bigger house ___so that___ (1.) we would have room for my parents. They're coming to the U.S. next month ________________ (2.) they want to be near us.

A: Don't you mind having your parents live with you?

B: Not at all. It'll be good for them and good for us. ________________ (3.) our jobs, we don't get home until after 6 p.m., and we don't want the kids to come home to an empty house.

A: Are your parents going to work?

B: No. They're not coming here ________________ (4.) jobs. They're in their late 60s and are both retired. They're coming here ________________ (5.) they can help out. But they're not just coming ________________ (6.) babysit. We want the kids to spend time with my parents ________________ (7.) they won't forget our language. Also, we want them to learn about our culture ________________ (8.) they've never been to our country. Our son is starting to speak more English than Spanish. He prefers English ________________ (9.) all his friends speak English.

A: That's how many kids are in America. They prefer to speak English ________________ (10.) they can be just like their friends. Do your parents speak English?

B: Just a little. What about your parents? Where do they live?

A: They live a few blocks away from me, but we almost never see each other ________________ (11.) our different schedules. ________________ (12.) they work in the day and I work in the evening, it's hard for us to get together.

EXERCISE 5 About You Fill in the blank with a reason or purpose. Discuss your answer with a partner.

1. I (or My family) decided to come to the U.S. ________________________________.

2. I (or We) chose this city ________________________________.

3. I (or We) plan/don't plan to go back ________________________________.

The LOST BOYS of SUDAN

Sudanese refugees and "Lost Boys" at a camp in Kenya

Read the following article. Pay special attention to the words in bold.

CD 2
TR 14

Besides immigrants, the United States takes in thousands of refugees a year. The Lost Boys of Sudan were children, living in southern Sudan in the late 1980s, when their long and difficult journey to the United States began. **While** these young boys were in the field taking care of their cattle,[3] their villages were attacked. These children, mostly boys between the ages of 4 and 12, ran for their lives. **For** three months, they walked hundreds of miles **until** they reached Ethiopia. They survived by eating leaves, roots, and wild fruit.

During that time, many died of starvation[4] and disease or were eaten by wild animals. Those who reached Ethiopia stayed in refugee camps **until** 1991, when a war started in Ethiopia and the camps were closed. They ran again, back to Sudan and then to Kenya, where they stayed in refugee camps **for** almost ten years. Of the approximately 27,000 boys who fled Sudan, only 11,000 survived.

During their time in the refugee camp, they got some schooling and learned basic English. In 1999, the United Nations and the U.S. government agreed to resettle 3,800 Lost Boys in the United States.

When they arrived in the United States, many challenges awaited them. They had to learn a completely new way of life. Many things were new for them: apartment living in a big city, strange foods, new technologies, and much more. **When** they saw an American supermarket for the first time, they were amazed by the amount of food. One boy was so surprised by the quantity of food in a supermarket that he asked if it was the palace of the king.

Agencies helped the Lost Boys with money for food and rent for a short time **until** they found jobs. **While** they were working, most of them enrolled in ESL classes. Now men, many have graduated from college and have started projects to help their villages back home. Peter Magai Bul, of Chicago, helped establish a school in his hometown. **While** he was studying for his college degree, Peter helped to raise funds for this school, which is currently educating over five hundred South Sudan students.

Although their future in the United States looks bright, **whenever** they think about their homeland, they are sad because so many of their family members and friends have died.

---

[3] *cattle:* cows, bulls, and oxen as a group

[4] *starvation:* the state of having no food, being extremely hungry

COMPREHENSION CHECK Based on the reading, tell if the statement is true (**T**) or false (**F**).

1. The Lost Boys were in a refugee camp in Ethiopia until they came to the U.S.
2. When their villages were attacked, the Lost Boys ran back home.
3. Some of the Lost Boys are helping their people in South Sudan.

9.3 Time Clauses and Phrases

Examples	Explanation
When their villages were attacked, the Lost Boys ran. Some young men will help their people back home **when** they finish college.	*When* means "at that time" or "immediately after that time." In a future sentence, we use the present in the time clause.
Whenever they think about their country, they are sad. **Whenever** they tell their story, Americans are amazed.	*Whenever* means "any time" or "every time."
They walked **until** they reached Ethiopia. They received money for a short time **until** they got jobs.	*Until* means "up to that time."
Peter has been a student **since** he came to the U.S. He has been working **(ever) since** he arrived in the U.S.	*Since* or *ever since* means "from that time in the past to the present." We use the present perfect or present perfect continuous in the main clause.
While they were taking care of their cattle, their villages were bombed. **As** they were coming to the U.S., they were thinking about their new life ahead.	We use *while* or *as* with a continuous action.
They walked **for** three months. They stayed in a refugee camp **for** many years.	We use *for* with an amount of time.
During the day, they walked. **During** their time in the refugee camp, they studied English.	We use *during* with a time such as *the day* or *summer*, or with a specific time period (*their time in Ethiopia, the month of August*) or an event (*the flight to the U.S.*).

EXERCISE 6 Fill in the blanks with *since, until, while, when, as, during, for,* or *whenever.* In some cases, more than one answer is possible.

1. The Lost Boys were very young ___when___ they left Sudan.
2. The Lost Boys walked ______________ many months.
3. ______________ their march to Ethiopia, many of them died.
4. They lived in Ethiopia ______________ about four years.

5. They crossed the river ________________ the rainy season.

6. Some died ________________ they were walking to Ethiopia.

7. They studied English ________________ they were living in Kenya.

8. ________________ they were traveling to the U.S., they were wondering about their future.

9. They had never seen a gas stove ________________ they came to the U.S.

10. ________________ they came to the U.S., they have had to learn many new things.

11. ________________ they came to the U.S., they saw modern appliances for the first time.

12. They enrolled in ESL classes ________________ they came to the U.S.

13. In the U.S. many of them worked ________________ they were going to school.

14. Peter has been working on his project back home ________________ 2004.

15. ________________ they think about their terrible journey, they feel sad.

EXERCISE 7 Fill in the blanks with an appropriate time word. In some cases, more than one answer is possible.

______When______ (1.) I was a child, I heard many stories about life in America. ____whenever____ (2.) I saw American movies, I dreamed about coming to the U.S. My uncle had lived in the U.S. ______for______ (3.) many years, and he often came back to visit. ____whenever\ when____ (4.) he came back, he used to tell me stories and show me pictures of the U.S. ______when______ (5.) I was a teenager, I asked my mother if she would let me visit my uncle ______during______ (6.) my summer vacation, but she said I was too young and the trip was too expensive. ______when______ (7.) I was 20, I finally decided to come to the U.S. ______while______ (8.) I was traveling to the U.S., I thought about all the stories my uncle had told me.

But I really knew nothing about the U.S. ______untill______ (9.) I came here. ______Since______ (10.) I came to the U.S., I've been working hard and trying to learn English. I haven't had time to meet Americans or have much fun ______Since______ (11.) I started my job. I've been here ______for______ (12.) five months now, and I just work and go to school. ______whenever______ (13.) I'm at school, I talk to my classmates ______during______ (14.) our break, but on the weekends I'm alone most of the time. I won't be able to make American friends ______until______ (15.) I learn more English.

EXERCISE 8 About You Write sentences about leaving your country and traveling to the U.S. or another country using the words given. Share your answers with a partner.

1. for

   For many years I wanted to leave my country. But my parents thought I was too young, so they wouldn't let me.

2. whenever

   ____

3. before

   ____

4. since

   ____

5. while

   ____

6. until

   ____

7. during

   ____

8. for

   ____

9. after

   ____

9.4 Using the *–ing* Form after Time Words

Examples
Subject / **Subject** The Lost Boys went to Ethiopia after **they left** Sudan. The Lost Boys went to Ethiopia after **leaving** Sudan.
Subject / **Subject** While **they were crossing** a river, some of the Lost Boys drowned. While **crossing** a river, some of the Lost Boys drowned.

Explanation
If the subject of the main clause and the subject of the time clause are the same, the sentence can be shortened by deleting the subject of the time clause and changing the verb to a present participle (*-ing*). Instead of a verb phrase, a participial phrase is used.

EXERCISE 9 Change the time clause to a participial phrase.

1. While they were running from their homes, they saw many dangerous animals.

   While running from their homes, they saw many dangerous animals.

2. The Lost Boys went to Kenya before they came to the U.S.

   " " " " " " " coming to the U.S.

3. While they were living in Kenya, they studied English.

   " living in Kenya, " " "

4. Before they came to the U.S., the Lost Boys had never used electricity.

   " coming " " " " " " " " "

5. Peter Bul learned how to use a computer after he came to the U.S.

   " " " " " " " " coming to the U.S

6. Before he found a job, Peter got help from the U.S. government.

   " finding a job, " " " " " " "

7. Peter went to visit South Sudan after he graduated from college.

   " " " " " " after graduating from college

8. While he was studying for his degree, Peter raised money for a school in South Sudan.

   While studying for his degree, " " " " " "

SLAVERY— An AMERICAN PARADOX[5]

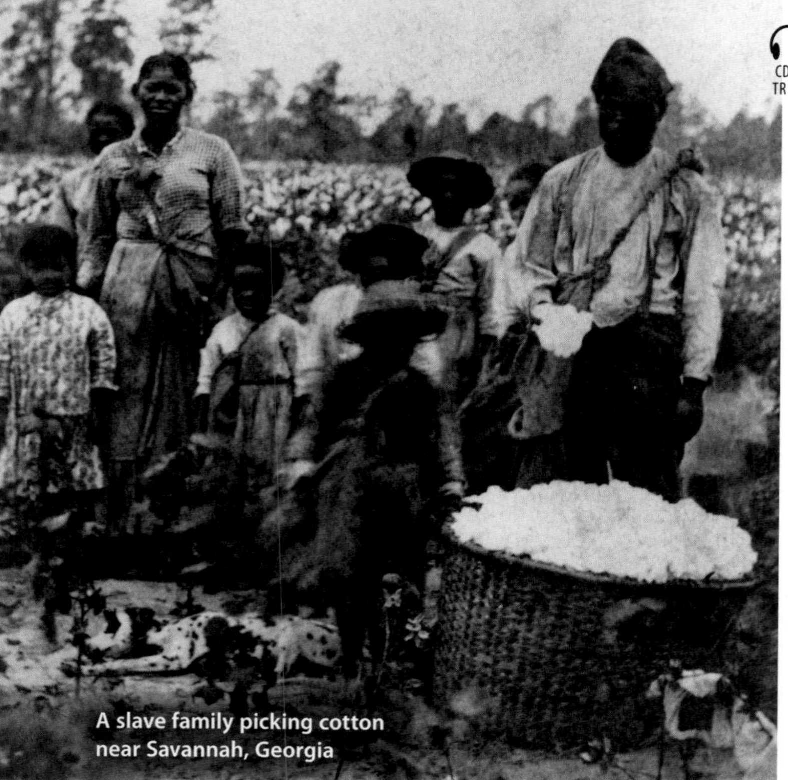
A slave family picking cotton near Savannah, Georgia

CD 2 TR 15 **Read the following article. Pay special attention to the words in bold.**

Even though most immigrants have come to the United States with great hopes and dreams, one group of people came unwillingly. They were taken as slaves from Africa. Almost half a million Africans were brought to work in the agricultural South. African families were torn apart as slaves were treated like property to be bought and sold.

In 1776, when the thirteen American colonies declared their independence from England, Thomas Jefferson, one of the founding fathers of the United States, wrote, "All men are created equal" and that every person has a right to "life, liberty, and the pursuit of happiness." **In spite of** these great words, Jefferson owned two hundred slaves. The newly formed U.S. Constitution considered each slave to be three-fifths of a person. In order to keep slaves divided from each other and dependent on their masters, they were prohibited from learning to read and write.

Since the main southern crop, tobacco, was exhausting the land at the end of the eighteenth century, it seemed that the need for slavery would come to an end. However, there was suddenly a big demand for cotton. Previously, the production of cotton had been very slow because it was very time-consuming to remove the seeds. But a new invention made the production of cotton much faster. Suddenly, southern farmers found a new area of wealth—and a new reason to keep slaves. **Even though** the African slave trade ended in 1808, domestic slave trade continued. The slave population continued to grow as children were born to slave mothers. By 1860, there were four million slaves in the United States.

The country became divided over the issue of slavery, and the Civil War, between the North and the South, was fought from 1861 to 1865. **In spite of the fact that** the North won and African Americans were freed, it took another hundred years for Congress to pass a law prohibiting discrimination because of race, color, religion, sex, or national origin. **In spite of** this law, discrimination still exists today.

Although many new arrivals see the United States as the land of equality, it is important to remember this dark period of American history.

---

[5] *paradox:* a situation that has contradictory aspects

COMPREHENSION CHECK Based on the reading, tell if the statement is true (**T**) or false (**F**).

1. The U.S. Constitution did not count slaves as part of the population.
2. Thomas Jefferson owned slaves.
3. When the slaves were freed, they gained equality.

9.5 Contrast

Examples	Explanation
Even though African slave trade ended, domestic slave trade continued. **Although** the U.S. Constitution guaranteed freedom, many African Americans weren't free. **In spite of the fact that** Jefferson wrote about equality, he owned slaves.	For an unexpected result or contrast of ideas, we use a clause beginning with *even though, although,* or *in spite of the fact that.*
In spite of the difficulties, the Lost Boys started a new life in the U.S.	We use *in spite of* + a noun (phrase) to show contrast.
Although the Lost Boys are happy in the U.S., they **still** miss their country. **Even though** it's hard to start a new life in a different country, many immigrants do it **anyway**.	In speech and informal writing, *still* and *anyway* can be used in the main clause to emphasize the contrast.

Language Note:

1. Informally, *even though* and *although* can be shortened to *though.*

   Though it was difficult, I adjusted to life in a new country.

2. In speech, *though* is often used at the end of a statement to show contrast with the preceding statement. (We don't use *even though* and *although* at the end of a statement.)

   I adjusted to life in a new country. It was difficult, **though.**

3. *While* is also used to show contrast. (Remember: *While* can also be a time word. The context tells you whether it shows time or contrast.)

   While it's not hard to understand slavery from an economic perspective, it's difficult for me to comprehend how people could have been so cruel to others.

EXERCISE 10 Circle the correct words to complete the conversation. If both choices are possible, circle both of them.

A: Are you surprised by slavery in the U.S.?

B: (*Even though/In spite of*)₁ I've read about it and seen movies about it, it's hard for me to understand. I've always thought of the U.S. as a land of freedom and opportunity, (*although/in spite of*)₂ I know it's not perfect. But slavery was so terrible. How could that have happened in the U.S.?

A: I rented a movie recently about an African American man in the North who was kidnapped in the 1800s and taken to the South. (*In spite of the fact that/Even though*)₃ he was a free man, he was sold into slavery.

The name of the movie is *12 Years a Slave.*

B: (*Although/In spite of*) **4.** I saw it a few years ago, I remember it well. (*In spite of/In spite of the fact that*) **5.** it was a wonderful movie, it was very hard to watch the cruel way slaves were treated.

A: Do you think it was a realistic movie?

B: Unfortunately, it was. In fact, the reality was probably even worse than what we saw in the movie.

EXERCISE 11 Fill in the blanks with *in spite of* or *in spite of the fact that.*

1. __In spite of the fact that__ the law says everyone has equal rights, some people are still suffering.
2. __In spite of__ Thomas Jefferson's declaration of equality for all, he owned slaves.
3. __In spite of the fact that__ slavery ended in 1865, African Americans did not receive equal treatment under the law until 1964.
4. The slave population continued to grow __in spite of the fact that__ Americans stopped importing slaves from Africa.
5. Many immigrants come to America __in spite of__ the difficulty of starting a new life.
6. The Lost Boys did not lose hope for a bright future __in spite of the fact that__ the challenges they faced.
7. __In spite of__ his busy schedule, Peter always tries to help his village in South Sudan.
8. __In spite of the fact that__ everything in America was new for them, the Lost Boys have adapted well to life in the U.S.
9. Many people still believe in the American dream __in spite of the fact that__ life is not perfect in the U.S.

EXERCISE 12 Circle the correct words to complete the paragraph. If both choices are possible, circle both of them.

When I was 16 years old, I wanted to come to the U.S. (*Even/Even though*) **1.** I was very young, my parents gave me permission to leave home and live with my uncle in New Jersey. (*In spite of the fact that/In spite of*) **2.** I was only in high school, I worked part-time and saved money for college. (*Although/In spite of*) **3.** it was hard, I managed to finish high school and start college. My uncle always encouraged me to go to college (*in spite of/even though*) **4.** he is not an educated man. A lot of my friends from high school didn't go to college (*even though/in spite of*) **5.** the opportunities they had. I decided to become an English teacher (*even though/although*) **6.** I still have a bit of an accent.

The Changing Face of the UNITED STATES

Read the following article. Pay special attention to the words in bold.

CD 2 TR 16

As of 2014, the U.S. population was over 319 million. This number is expected to rise to more than 438 million by 2050. Most of the population growth will be from immigrants and their descendants. **Unless** there are changes in immigration patterns, nearly one in five people will be an immigrant in 2050. This is even higher than the top figures between 1890 and 1910, when about 15 percent were foreign born. Of course, these numbers assume that the immigration policy in the U.S. will remain the way it is now.

For most of the nineteenth and twentieth centuries, the majority of immigrants to the U.S. were Europeans. However, since 1970, this trend has changed dramatically. More than 50 percent of the immigrants who have arrived since 1970 are Spanish speakers. In 2003, Hispanics passed African Americans as the largest minority. The Hispanic population increased more than 50 percent between 1990 and 2000. **If** current patterns of immigration continue and **if** the birth rate remains the same, Hispanics, who are now 17 percent of the total population, will be 29 percent of the population by 2050. Hispanics are already about 38 percent of the population of California and Texas.

Because of their increasing numbers, Hispanic voters are gaining political power. In 2008, President Obama received 67 percent of the Hispanic vote. In 2012, when Hispanics made up 10 percent of the voting population, Obama received 71 percent of their vote. It is clear that Hispanics have the power to determine elections.

Even if immigration policy changes, Hispanics, who have a higher birth rate than other Americans, will continue to see their numbers—and influence—grow.

There are many questions about the future of America. One thing is certain: the face of America is changing.

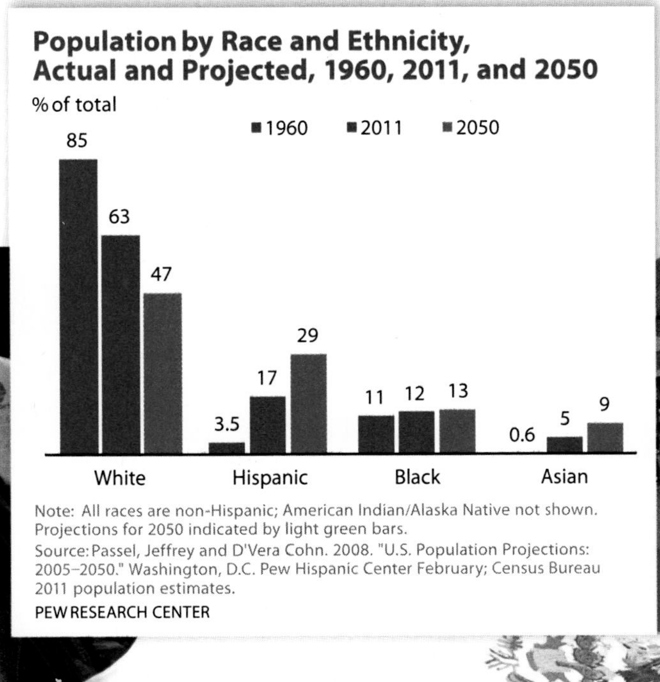

A Cinco de Mayo celebration in Detroit

COMPREHENSION CHECK Based on the reading, tell if the statement is true (**T**) or false (**F**).

1. African Americans are the largest minority in the U.S. today.
2. By the middle of this century, 50 percent of the population will be Hispanic.
3. Hispanics helped determine the presidential elections of 2008 and 2012.

9.6 Condition

Examples	Explanation
If Hispanics **vote** together, they **will have** a lot of political power.	We use *if* to show that the condition affects the result.
Even if the immigration of Hispanics **slows** down, their number **will** probably **increase**.	We use *even if* to show that the condition doesn't affect the result.
You don't have political power **unless** you vote.	We use *unless* to mean *if not. You don't have political power if you don't vote.*

Language Note:

If, even if, and *unless* can be used with present, past, and future sentences. In a future sentence, we use the simple present in the condition clause.

EXERCISE 13 Fill in the blanks with the correct form of the verb given.

1. If the Hispanic population ___continues___ (a. continue) to grow, 29 percent of the U.S. population ___will be___ (b. be) Hispanic by the year 2050.
2. Even if the number of immigrants __________ (a. go) down, the general population __________ (b. increase).
3. If more children __________ (a. be) born in the next 50 years, more schools __________ (b. passive: need).
4. School classes __________ (a. get) bigger if the number of school-age children __________ (b. increase).
5. The U.S. population __________ (a. be) almost 440 million by 2050 if immigration __________ (b. continue) at the same rate.
6. Children of immigrants __________ (a. forget) their native language unless their parents __________ (b. encourage) them to speak it.

EXERCISE 14 Change the *if* clause in the sentences below to an *unless* clause.

1. Immigrants can't become American citizens if they don't pass a test.

   Immigrants can't become American citizens unless they pass a test.

2. Visitors can't enter the U.S. if they don't have a passport.

Visitors can't enter the U.S. unless they have a passport

3. Immigrants will continue to come to the U.S. if conditions in their native countries don't improve.

Immigrant will continue to come to the U.S. unless conditions in thier countries improve.

4. In the 1800s, Southern farmers couldn't prosper if they didn't find a new crop to grow.

In the 1800s, Southern farmers couldn't prosper unless they find a new corp to grow

5. Cotton production was going to be slow if they didn't have a machine to help.

Cotton production was going to be slow unless they had a machine to help

6. Foreigners cannot work in the U.S. if they don't have permission.

Foreigners cannot work in the U.S. unless they have permission.

EXERCISE 15 Fill in the blanks in this conversation. Use *if* or *unless*.

A: My youngest daughter is seven years old, and she doesn't speak Spanish anymore. ___If___ (1.) I say something to her in Spanish, she understands, but she answers in English.

B: ___If___ (2.) all her friends speak English, of course she's going to speak English.

A: My mother lives with us. She doesn't speak English. She can't understand what my daughter is saying ___Unless___ (3.) I translate it for her.

B: I have the same problem. My son is 14 and he won't speak Spanish ___unless___ (4.) he has to. Last month my parents came to visit from Guatemala. My parents had a hard time understanding my son because he mixes Spanish and English. There are a lot of Spanish words he doesn't remember ___unless___ (5.) I remind him.

A: Maybe we should put our kids in a bilingual program at school. ___If___ (6.) they're in the bilingual program, they'll have to speak Spanish.

B: I don't think the school will put them in a bilingual program ___unless___ (7.) they're already fluent in English.

A: We can't fight it. Our kids won't speak Spanish well ___unless___ (8.) we go back to live in our native countries.

EXERCISE 16 About You Fill in the blanks and discuss your answers with a partner.

1. My English won't improve quickly unless ____________________
2. People understand my English even if ____________________
3. If ____________________, people don't understand me well.

EXERCISE 17 Fill in the blanks to complete this conversation between a Colombian woman who's going to immigrate to the U.S. and her friend. Use context clues to help you. Answers may vary.

A: I'm planning to go to Boston. I'm worried about the weather. They say it's very cold in the winter.

B: I'm sure people go out even if *the weather is cold* (1.).

A: What if people won't understand me? My accent isn't perfect.

B: Even if ____________________ (2.), people will probably understand you.

A: But I make so many grammar mistakes.

B: Don't worry. People will understand you even if ____________________ (3.). Are you planning to get a job there?

A: I don't think I'm going to need one. I'm going to live with my relatives and they said I can live there for free.

B: Even if ____________________ (4.), you'll need money for other things, like books, clothes, and transportation.

A: I know college is going to be expensive for me because I'm going to be an international student. I think college is free for American residents, isn't it?

B: No. Even if ____________________ (5.), you have to pay for college, but it's cheaper for residents.

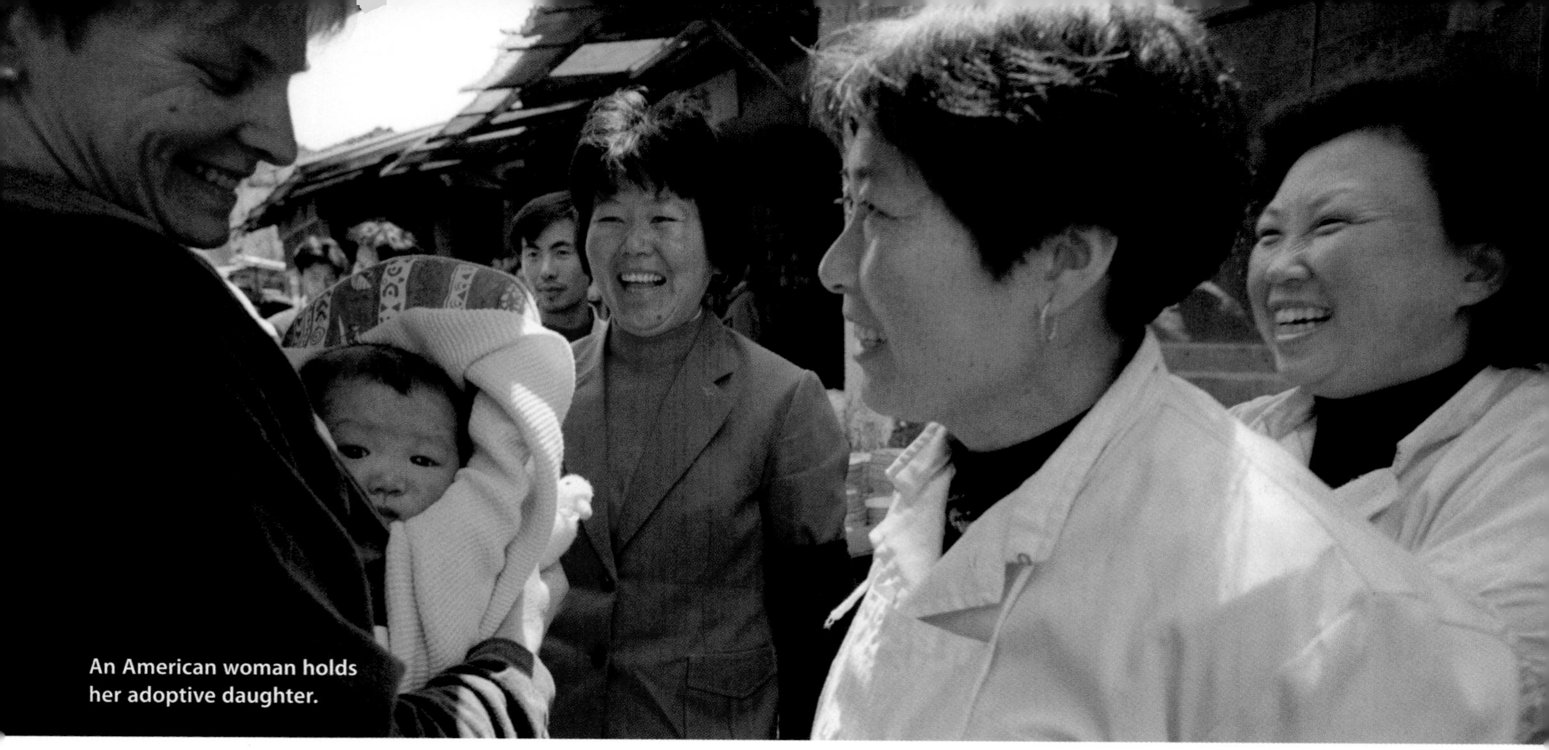

An American woman holds her adoptive daughter.

ADOPTING a BABY from ABROAD

CD 2 TR 17

Read the following article. Pay special attention to the words in bold.

Many American couples want to adopt children. **However**, the adoption of an American child is a long and complicated process. There are so few babies available for adoption in the United States that parents who want an American baby often have to wait years. **As a result**, many Americans turn to foreign countries for adoption. In 2009, 13,000 foreign babies were adopted from 106 countries by American families. Americans bring home babies from many countries, with the majority coming from China, Ethiopia, Ukraine, and South Korea.

The process of foreign adoption takes time and patience. **First**, the United States Citizenship and Immigration Services (USCIS) must determine if a family can provide a loving, stable home for the child. Social workers do a home study on each family. They give the USCIS a family's personal, financial, and medical information. **Also**, there are many forms to fill out and documents to produce to complete the process. **For example**, the family has to show proof of health insurance.

In addition, foreign adoption is not cheap. **In fact**, the average cost of an international adoption in 2009 was $44,000. **Furthermore**, parents have the expense of traveling to the country and staying there for many weeks while the process is being completed.

In spite of all these difficulties, these tiny immigrants bring joy to many American families.

COMPREHENSION CHECK Based on the reading, tell if the statement is true (**T**) or false (**F**).

1. Adopting a baby from abroad is very expensive.
2. When the family returns with the child, a home study is done.
3. If a family adopts a baby from abroad, they have to go to the foreign country to pick up the baby.

9.7 Sentence Connectors

Sentence connectors[6] show the relationship between ideas.

Examples	Explanation
Some couples want to adopt American children. **However**, there are very few babies available in the U.S. Some couples want to adopt a baby from abroad. **Nevertheless**, the process isn't cheap or easy.	Sentence connectors that show contrast are *however* and *nevertheless*. These words are similar in meaning to *but*.
Foreign adoption is not for everyone. It can be expensive. **In addition**, it can take a long time. Adopting a baby from abroad is expensive. Parents have to pay the adoption agencies. **Furthermore**, they have the expense of traveling to pick up the baby.	Sentence connectors that add more information to the same idea are *in addition, furthermore, also,* and *moreover*. These words are similar in meaning to *and*.
Adoptive parents have many things to do. **First**, they have to fill out an application. **Next**, they have to produce many documents. **Furthermore**, they need to have a home study done.	Ideas can be ordered using *first, second, third, next, then,* etc. We can begin with *first* and continue with *furthermore, moreover, also, in addition.*
It takes a long time to adopt an American baby. **As a result**, many Americans go to foreign countries to adopt. Many couples in China prefer sons. **Therefore**, the majority of adoptions from China are girls.	Sentence connectors that show result or conclusion are *therefore, as a result*, and *for this reason*. These words are similar in meaning to *so*.
Adoptive families have to produce many documents. **For example**, they have to show proof of health insurance. Foreign adoption is not cheap. **In fact**, the average cost was $44,000 in 2009.	Other connectors are *for example* and *in fact*. *In fact* emphasizes the preceding statement. Sometimes it introduces something that might surprise the reader or listener.

Punctuation Notes:

1. We use either a period or a semicolon (;) before a sentence connector if it comes at the beginning of a sentence. We use a comma after a sentence connector.

   My friends couldn't adopt a baby here. **Therefore**, they went to another country to adopt.

   My friends couldn't adopt a baby here; **therefore**, they went to another country to adopt.

2. Some sentence connectors can come in the middle of a sentence. We separate these from the sentence by putting a comma before and after the connector.

   Many people want to adopt a baby. The process, **however**, is not cheap or easy.

[6] The grammatical name for these connectors is conjunctive adverbs.

EXERCISE 18 Choose the correct sentence connectors to fill in the blanks. In some cases both choices are possible, so circle both options.

1. The Lost Boys were happy living with their families in Sudan. (*However*/*In addition*), a war forced them to leave.
2. The Lost Boys faced many problems when they left Sudan. They didn't know where to go. (*Furthermore/Moreover*), they didn't have enough to eat.
3. Some of them couldn't swim. (*As a result/However*), some drowned when they had to cross a river in their escape.
4. Finally they found safety in a refugee camp in Kenya. (*However/In fact*), conditions in the camp were very poor.
5. Many of the Lost Boys had never seen modern appliances before. (*Also/For example*), they had never used a gas stove.
6. They faced problems in the U.S. They had to find jobs quickly. (*For example/In addition*), they had to go to school to improve their English.
7. They are happy that they came to the U.S. (*In fact/Nevertheless*), they still miss their family and friends back home.
8. Jews had a hard life in Eastern Europe. Many lived in poor conditions. (*Moreover/However*), they suffered religious persecution.
9. My grandfather immigrated to the U.S. for several reasons. (*First/In addition*), he needed to find a job to make more money. (*In fact/Furthermore*), he wanted to be reunited with his relatives who had come before him.
10. There was a big famine in Ireland. (*As a result/For this reason*), many Irish people left and came to the U.S.
11. Many people wanted to escape political problems in their countries. (*However/For example*), some of them couldn't get permission to come to the U.S.
12. A war broke out in Yugoslavia in 1992. (*As a result/For example*), many people died or lost their homes.
13. Most immigrants have come to the U.S. because they wanted to. (*However/Furthermore*), Africans were brought to America against their will to work as slaves.
14. In 1776, Thomas Jefferson wrote, "All men are created equal." (*Nevertheless/Therefore*), Jefferson had 200 slaves at that time.
15. Members of the same African family were sent to different areas to work as slaves. (*Therefore/As a result*), families were torn apart.
16. Slavery officially ended in 1865. (*However/Consequently*), many African American families continued to suffer.
17. African Americans had been the largest minority for many years. (*In fact/However*), this changed in 2003 when the Hispanic population became the largest minority.
18. Adopting a foreign baby is complicated. People have to pay a lot of money. (*Moreover/Furthermore*), they have to travel to the foreign country to fill out forms and pick up the baby.
19. The U.S. started to have serious economic problems in 2008. (*However/Consequently*), some foreigners were afraid to immigrate because they thought they wouldn't find jobs.
20. The U.S. attracts more immigrants than any other country. (*In fact/For example*), one in five of the world's immigrants lives in the U.S.

EXERCISE 19 Complete each statement. Answers will vary.

1. The U.S. is a rich country. However, it has many poor people. Unemployment is high and many people don't have jobs.
2. It is important for me to learn English. Therefore, ____________________
3. It is important for me to learn English. However, ____________________
4. Living in another country is difficult. Immigrants have to adjust to a new language. In addition, ____________________
5. Some children speak one language at home and another at school. As a result, ____________________
6. To learn a new language, you must master the grammar. In addition, ____________________
7. No one wants to leave friends and family. However, ____________________
8. If someone wants to come to the U.S. to visit, he or she must have a passport. In addition, ____________________
9. It's important for a new immigrant to know English. Therefore, ____________________

10. I don't speak English perfectly. However, ____

____

____

11. English is not the only language of the U.S. In fact, ________________________________

____

____

12. Life is hard for recent immigrants. First, ______________________________________. Then,

____

____

13. Some immigrants don't learn English quickly. For example, ____________________________

____

____

9.8 *So . . . That / Such . . . That*

Examples	Explanation
Foreign adoption is **such a long process that** people often become impatient. The Lost Boys saw **such terrible things that** they will never forget them.	We use: *such* + *a/an* + adjective + singular noun + *that* *such* + adjective + plural noun + *that*
Foreign adoption is **so expensive that** many people cannot afford it. Children of immigrants learn English **so easily that** they become fluent in a short time.	We use: *so* + adjective + *that* *so* + adverb + *that*
In Miami, there are **so many Spanish speakers that** you can hear Spanish wherever you go. There are **so few American babies** available for adoption **that** many Americans adopt foreign babies.	We use: *so many* + plural count noun + *that* *so few* + plural count noun + *that*
There was **so much poverty** in Ireland in the 1800s **that** many people were forced to leave the country. The Lost Boys had **so little food** to eat **that** many of them died.	We use: *so much* + noncount noun + *that* *so little* + noncount noun + *that*

Language Note:

That is often omitted in informal speech.

Peter works **so hard** (*that*) he doesn't have time to rest.

EXERCISE 20 Fill in the blanks with *so, so much, so many, so few, so little,* or *such (a/an).*

1. We had ___so many___ problems in our country that we decided to leave.
2. I waited ______________ long time that I thought I would never get permission.
3. When I got to the airport, the security lines were ______________ long that I had to wait for 2 hours.
4. There were ______________ people arriving at the same time that the process took a long time.
5. I was ______________ happy when I got my Green Card that I started to cry.
6. The U.S. offers ______________ freedom that people from all over the world want to come here.
7. Before I got my visa, I had to fill out ______________ papers and give ______________ information that I thought I would never be able to do it.
8. We have been in the U.S. for ______________ long time that we hardly speak our native language anymore.
9. My neighbor's daughter was ______________ young when she arrived from China that she doesn't remember anything about China at all.
10. There are ______________ American babies to adopt that many families adopt babies from abroad.
11. I spoke ______________ English when I arrived in the U.S. that I always had to take my dictionary with me everywhere.

EXERCISE 21 Fill in the blanks with *so, so much, so many, so little, so few,* or *such a.* Then complete each statement with a result. Answers will vary.

1. I was ______________ happy when I got permission to come to the U.S. that ______________ ______________.
2. Most adopted children are ______________ young when they come to the U.S. that ______________ ______________.
3. Some people have ______________ hard time learning English in the U.S. that ______________ ______________.
4. Some people had ______________ hard life in their native countries that ______________ ______________.
5. In 1910, there were ______________ foreign-born Americans that ______________ ______________.
6. I had ______________ time to prepare for that trip that ______________.

SUMMARY OF LESSON 9

1. Words that connect a dependent clause or phrase to an independent clause: *(Abbreviations: C = Clause; NP = Noun Phrase; VP = Verb Phrase; PP = Participial Phrase)*

Function	Connectors	Examples
Reason	*because* + C	**Because** he studies hard, his English is improving.
	since + C	**Since** he studies hard, his English is improving.
	because of + NP	**Because of** his effort, his English is improving.
Time	*when* + C	They decided to adopt a Korean baby **when** they couldn't get an American baby.
	whenever + C	**Whenever** they have a chance, they visit Korea.
	until + C or NP	The baby lived in an orphanage **until** she was adopted. The baby lived in Korea **until** May.
	while + C or PP	**While** they were traveling to the U.S., they were thinking about the baby's future. **While** traveling to the U.S., they were holding their new baby.
	for + NP	They stayed in Korea **for** 3 weeks.
	during + NP	They went to Korea **during** the summer.
	since + NP or C	The baby has been living in the U.S. **since** June. The baby has been living in the U.S. **since** the family brought her here.
Purpose	*(in order) to* + VP	He came to the U.S. **(in order) to** have a better life.
	so (that) + C	He came to the U.S. **so (that)** he could improve his life.
	for + NP	He came to the U.S. **for** a better education.
Contrast	*even though* + C	**Even though** life was difficult for them, the Lost Boys didn't lose hope.
	although + C	**Although** life was difficult for them, the Lost Boys didn't lose hope.
	in spite of the fact that + C	**In spite of the fact that** life was difficult for them, the Lost Boys didn't lose hope.
	in spite of + NP	**In spite of** the difficulties, the Lost Boys didn't lose hope.
Condition	*if* + C	**If** population growth continues in the same way, the U.S. will have 438 million people by 2050.
	even if + C	**Even if** immigration slows, the population will increase.
	unless + C	**Unless** there are changes in population patterns, one in five people in the U.S. will be an immigrant by 2050.

2. Words that connect two independent clauses:

Function	Connectors	Examples
To add more to the same idea	*in addition* *furthermore* *moreover*	Adopting a baby from abroad is not easy. Parents have to pay a lot of money. **In addition**, officials need to approve of their home life.
To add a contrasting idea	*however* *nevertheless*	The law says that everyone is equal. **However**, inequalities still exist.
To show a result	*therefore* *as a result* *for this reason* *consequently*	Some people suffer economic hardships. **Therefore**, they want to leave their countries.
To give an example	*for example*	Besides learning English, the Lost Boys faced many challenges when they arrived in the U.S. **For example**, they had to learn about city life.
To emphasize the truth of the preceding statement	*in fact*	The Lost Boys didn't see their parents for many years. **In fact**, they didn't even know if their parents were dead or alive.

3. Words that introduce result clauses:

Function	Connectors	Examples
Result	• *so* + adjective + *that* • *so* + adverb + *that* • *so many* + plural noun + *that* • *so few* + plural noun + *that* • *so much* + noncount noun + *that* • *so little* + noncount noun + *that* • *such a/an* + adjective + singular noun + *that* • *such* + adjective + plural noun + *that*	She was **so sad** to leave her country **that** she cried. He speaks English **so fluently that** everyone thinks it's his first language. Adopting a baby costs **so much money that** many people can't do it. The Lost Boys had **such a difficult time that** many died.

Circle the correct words to complete this story. If both choices are correct, circle both.

Many people have come to America (*because/for*) freedom. But between the 1600s and the early 1800s, Africans were brought to America against their will (*for/to*) work in the fields of the South. Africans were taken from their homes and put on slave ships (*for/to*) cross the Atlantic. Conditions were (*so/such*) hard that many died along the way.
1. 2. 3. 4.

Working conditions on the farms were terrible too. (*For example/Also*), slaves had to pick cotton in the hot southern sun all day. They worked hard from morning till night (*so that/in order to*) plantation owners could become rich. These owners were often cruel to their slaves. (*In fact/However*), they often beat their slaves who didn't obey. (*In addition/Furthermore*), they provided only a minimum of food for survival.
5. 6. 7. 8.

(*Although/Unless*) many people in the North were against slavery, slavery continued in the South (*because of/since*) Southern slave owners did not want to give up their cheap labor supply.
9. 10.

(*Even though/However,*) an 1808 law prohibited the importation of slaves, slavery continued. (*In fact/In spite of*), by 1860, there were 4 million slaves in America. (*In spite of/In spite of the fact that*) the difficulties of living under slavery, slaves formed strong communities. They tried to preserve their African cultural practices, which included music and dance. (*Because/For*) people from the same regions in Africa were separated from each other, they lost their native languages, used English, and were given names by their owners.
11. 12. 13. 14.

Most people of African descent in the North were free. (*In addition/However*), they didn't have an easy life. They couldn't attend public schools. (*Furthermore/However*), they weren't allowed to vote. Many slaves from the South tried to run away to the North. (*However,/Although*) some were caught and sent back to their owners.
15. 16. 17.

(*Unless/Until*) the slaves were finally freed in 1865, they faced many difficulties. (*In spite of the fact that/In spite of*) the majority of Africans by that time were born in America, they suffered discrimination (*because/because of*) the color of their skin.
18. 19. 20.

Discrimination was still legal (*when/until*) 1964, when Congress passed a law prohibiting discrimination in jobs and education. (*Although/In spite of*) there has been progress toward equality for all, there are still many inequalities in American life.
21. 22.

WRITING

PART 1 Editing Advice

1. Use *to*, not *for*, with a verb when showing purpose.

    She came to the U.S. ~~for~~ to get a better education.

2. Don't combine *so* with *because*, or *but* with *even though*.

    Because his country was at war, ~~so~~ he left his country.

    Even though he speaks English well, ~~but~~ he can't find a job.

3. Use *because of* when a noun phrase follows.

    People don't understand me well because ^of my accent.

4. Don't use *even* without *though* or *if* to introduce a clause.

    Even ^though Peter misses his family, he's happy in the U.S.

5. Use the *-ing* form, not the base form, after a time word if the subject is deleted.

    Before ~~come~~ coming to the U.S., he studied English.

6. Don't confuse *so that* (purpose) with *so* (result).

    She wanted to have a better life, so ~~that~~ she came to the U.S.

7. After *so that*, use a modal before the verb.

    Farmers used slave labor so that they ^could become rich.

8. In a future sentence, use the simple present in the *if* clause or time clause.

    If I ~~will~~ go back to my hometown, I will tell my family about life in the U.S.

9. *However* connects two sentences. *Although* connects two parts of the same sentence.

    I studied English in my country. ~~Although~~ However, I didn't understand Americans when I arrived.

10. An adverbial clause or phrase must be attached to the main clause.

    She went to Canada because her parents were living there.
    ~~She went to Canada. Because her parents were living there.~~

11. Use *so* + adjective/adverb. Use *such* when you include a noun.

    It was ~~so~~ such a long and boring trip to the U.S. that I slept most of the way. *OR*
    The trip to the U.S. was so long and boring that I slept most of the way.

12. Use correct punctuation with sentence connectors.

    She likes living here~~, h~~. However, she misses her family back home.

PART 2 Editing Practice

Some of the shaded words and phrases have mistakes. Find the mistakes and correct them. If the shaded words are correct, write *C*.

Life as an immigrant can be hard. I came to the U.S. five years ago for [1.] study English. I chose to live in this city because [2.] my sister was living here. Even [3.] I had studied English in my country, I didn't have experience talking with native speakers. I wanted to prepare myself, therefore [4.], I took private lessons with an American in my country for [5.] learn American expressions. In addition [6.], before come [7.] here, I read a lot about life in the U.S. so that I was [8.] prepared. But I wasn't. There were many surprises. For example [9.], I was surprised by how cold it is in the winter in this city. Therefore [10.], I couldn't believe that some students call their teachers by their first names. Back home, we always call our teachers "Professor" for [11.] show respect. I also miss getting together with friends after class. Now I'm at a city college and most students have jobs and families. As a result [12.], everyone leaves after class. Because [13.] they want to get home to their families. I gave my phone number to some classmates so that we get together [14.] on weekends, but no one ever calls me. I thought I wouldn't be lonely since [15.] I'd be with my sister and her family. But I was wrong. Because my sister has a busy life, so [16.] she doesn't have much time for me either.

I had so [17.] hard time when I arrived here that [18.] I wanted to go back. Even though [19.], little by little I got used to life here. I discovered that church is a good place to meet people, so that [20.] I joined a church. When I will save [21.] more money, I'm going to get an apartment with one of my new friends from church. Even though life has become easier, but [22.] I still miss my family back home.

PART 3 Write About It

1. Describe the problems or challenges immigrants or refugees can face when they arrive in the U.S.
2. Describe the challenges international students can face when they become students in the U.S.

PART 4 Edit Your Writing

Reread the Summary of Lesson 9 and the editing advice. Edit your writing from Part 3.

LESSON

10 Noun Clauses

CHILDREN

Children peer out a window in Lubljana, Slovenia

Children must be taught how to think,
not what to think.

—Margaret Mead

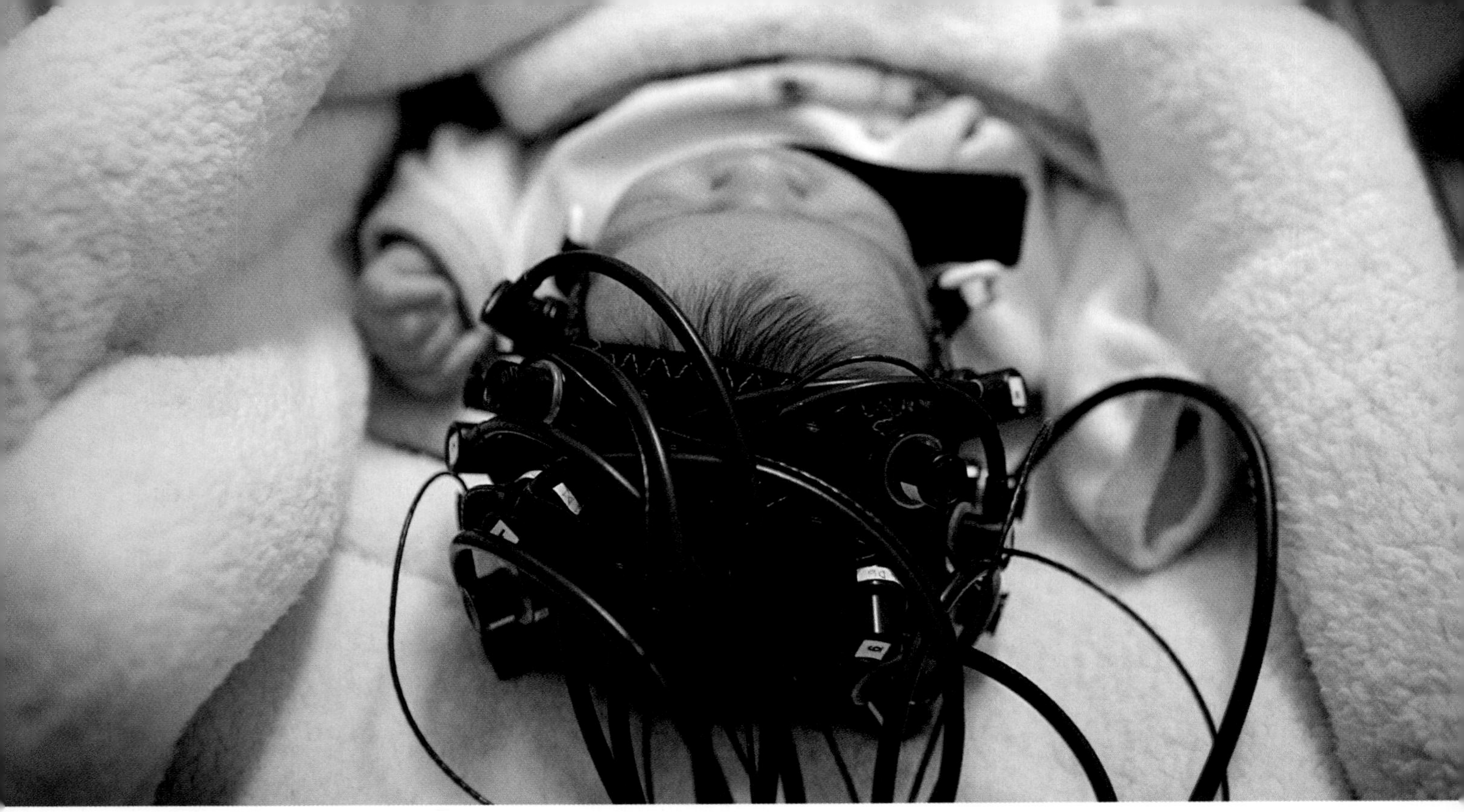

A brain imaging method that measures brain activity is applied to newborns to study early perception of speech and the ability to learn syntactically.

EARLY **CHILD** DEVELOPMENT

CD 2
TR 18

Read the following article. Pay special attention to the words in bold.

Do you think **that babies can benefit from listening to classical music or seeing great works of art**? Some parents think **that these activities can increase a baby's intelligence**. While there is no scientific evidence to support this, research shows **that a baby's early experiences influence brain development**. The first three years of a baby's life affect his emotional development and learning abilities for the rest of his life. It is a well-known fact **that talking to infants increases their language ability** and **that reading to them is the most important thing parents can do to raise a good reader**. A recent study shows **that children from birth to eight years old are spending much more time with screens than books**.

Babies whose parents rarely talk to them or hold them can be damaged for life. One study shows **that kids who hardly play or who aren't touched very much develop brains 20 to 50 percent smaller than normal**.

A recent study at the University of North Carolina followed children from preschool to young adulthood. The results showed **that children who got high-quality preschool education from the time they were infants benefited in later life**. In this study, 23 percent of children who had high-quality preschool education graduated from college, compared with only 6 percent of children who did not have preschool education.

While it is important to give babies stimulating activities, experts warn **that parents shouldn't overstimulate them**.

COMPREHENSION CHECK Based on the reading, tell if the statement is true (**T**) or false (**F**).

1. If a baby listens to classical music, this will help develop his brain.
2. Reading to babies helps them become better readers.
3. The first three years of children's lives affect their learning for the rest their lives.

10.1 Noun Clauses

A noun clause has a subject and a verb. It functions as a noun in a sentence.

Examples	Explanation
Parents know **(that) kids need a lot of attention.** Studies show **(that) early childhood education is important**.	A noun clause can follow certain verbs. *That* introduces a noun clause. *That* is often omitted, especially in conversation.
I'm sure **(that) children need a lot of attention**. Some parents are worried **(that) they don't spend enough time with their kids**.	A noun clause can be the complement of the sentence after certain adjectives.
A: I hope **that our children will be successful.** **B:** I hope **so** too. **A:** Do you think **that the children are learning in pre-school**? **B:** Yes, I think **so**.	Noun clauses can be replaced by *so* after the verbs *think, hope, believe, suppose, expect,* and *know.*
I realize that the child is tired **and that** he hasn't eaten lunch. I know that you are a loving parent **but that** you can't spend much time with your child.	Connect two noun clauses in the same sentence with *and that* or *but that.*

Language Notes:

1. A noun clause often follows one of these verbs:

believe	find out	predict	suppose
complain	forget	pretend	think
decide	hope	realize	understand
dream	know	regret	
expect	learn	remember	
feel*	notice	show	

* *Feel* followed by a noun clause means "believe" or "think."

I *feel* that early education is important. = I *believe/think* that early education is important.

2. A noun clause often follows *be* + the following adjectives:

afraid	clear	sure
amazed	disappointed	surprised
aware	glad	worried
certain	happy	

EXERCISE 1 Listen to the following conversation. Fill in the blanks with the words you hear.

CD 2
TR 19

A: Do you know that (1.) it's good to read to children when they're very young?

B: Yes, I do. But ________ (2.) playing music was important too.

A: ________ (3.) that music is beneficial, but I suppose it can't hurt.

B: ________ (4.) it's good to give kids as much education as possible before they go to school.

A: I'm sure that's a good idea. But ________ (5.) they're just kids. They need to play too.

B: Of course they do. ________ (6.) my children will be successful one day.

A: ________ (7.) they'll be very successful and happy.

B: ________ (8.).

EXERCISE 2 Fill in the blanks to complete the noun clause based on the reading on page 282. Answers may vary.

1. Research shows that a baby's early experiences influence his brain development.
2. A recent study shows that children are spending much more time with screen than reading books.
3. Some parents think that it's important to play classical music for babies.
4. We all know that talking to infants and reading increases their language ability.
5. A study shows that kids who hardly play have smaller brains.

EXERCISE 3 Respond to each statistic[1] about American families by beginning with *I'm surprised that . . .* or *I'm not surprised that . . .* Discuss your reactions with a partner.

1. The number of children in the U.S. is increasing rapidly.

   I'm surprised that the number of children in the U.S. is increasing rapidly.

2. About 7 million American children are home alone after school.

   I'm amazed that about 7 million American children are home alone

3. About 22 percent of American children live in poverty.

   I'm disappointed that 22 percent of American children live in poverty.

4. About 70 percent of married mothers work outside the home.

   I'm not surprised that 70 percent of married mother work outside the home

[1] Source: http://www.childstats.gov

5. Sixty-nine percent of children live with two parents.

____

6. Twenty-three percent of American children live with at least one foreign-born parent.

____

7. Twenty-two percent of children ages five to seventeen speak a language other than English at home.

____

8. By 2050, 39 percent of U.S. children are projected to be Hispanic.

____

EXERCISE 4 About You Fill in the blanks with a noun clause to talk about families or raising children in the U.S. or your country. Discuss your answers with a partner.

1. I'm surprised ____.
2. I think ____.
3. I know ____.
4. It's unfortunate ____.
5. I'm not surprised ____.
6. I've noticed ____.

EXERCISE 5 About You What's your opinion? Answer the questions using *I think* and a noun clause. Discuss your answers with a partner.

1. Should the government help families pay for childcare while the parents work?
2. Can children get the care and attention they need in day care?
3. Should fathers take a greater part in raising their kids?
4. Should grandparents help more in raising their grandchildren?
5. Should employers give new mothers maternity leave? For how long?
6. Should parents read books to babies before they learn to talk?
7. Should parents buy a lot of toys for their children?

The TEENAGE BRAIN

CD 2 TR 20

Read the following article. Pay special attention to the words in bold.

For many American teenagers, sixteen is the magic number—the age when they can get their driver's license. But this is also the time when parents worry the most about their kids.

In the United States, one in three teen deaths is from a car crash. Parents often wonder **if kids really understand the risks they are taking when they are behind the wheel**. They warn their kids **what to do and what not to do** while driving, but they really don't know **whether their kids will follow their advice or not**. They hand over the car keys—and hope for the best.

Studies show that when teens drive alone, they take risks at the same rate as adults. But when they drive with other teens, they take more risks.

Scientists have been using scans[2] to study the teenage brain. Even though the brain is almost full size by the time a child is six years old, scientists are finding that the brain makes great changes between the ages of twelve and twenty-five. During this time, it is natural that young people seek thrills.[3] According to Laurence Steinberg, a developmental psychologist from Temple University, "The teenage brain is like a car with a good accelerator but a weak brake. . . . Adolescents are more impulsive,[4] thrill-seeking, drawn to the rewards of a risky decision than adults."

While new technologies can make driving more dangerous, there are other technologies that help parents keep track of their teenagers' driving habits. There are phone apps that let parents know **what their kids are doing behind the wheel**. Parents can know **if their child is texting or tweeting while driving** or **how fast their teenager is driving**.

Risky behavior is a normal stage of development in teenagers. "I can't stand riding on a roller-coaster now," said Professor Steinberg. "I liked it as a teenager. I can't stand driving fast now. I liked driving fast when I was a teenager. What has changed? I'm not as driven today by this thrill-seeking sensation."

---

2 *scans:* an examination of an inside part of the body done with a special machine
3 *thrill:* a feeling of strong excitement, or pleasure
4 *impulsive:* done with a sudden urge

A young driver practices driving.

COMPREHENSION CHECK Based on the reading, tell if the statement is true (**T**) or false (**F**).

1. When teenagers drive with other teenagers in the car, they take more risks.
2. The brain is fully developed by the age of twelve.
3. The majority of teen deaths are the result of car crashes.

10.2 Noun Clauses as Included Questions[5]

A noun clause is used to include a question in a statement or another question.

Direct Question	Included Question
Wh- questions with auxiliaries or ***be***	We use statement word order. Put the subject before the verb.
How fast is my daughter driving? What app can I use?	I'd like to know **how fast she is driving**. Please tell me **what app I can use**.
Wh- questions with auxiliaries or ***do/does/did***	We remove *do/does/did*. The verb shows **-s** ending for *he, she,* or *it,* or the past form.
Why does a teenager take risks? How did the car accident happen?	Scientists want to know **why a teenager takes risks**. I'd like to know **how the car accident happened**.
Wh- questions about the subject	There is no change in word order.
Who bought the app? What makes the teenage brain different?	I'd like to know **who bought the app**. Scientists want to know **what makes the teenage brain different**.
Yes/No questions with auxiliaries or ***be***	We add the word *if* or *whether.* We use statement word order. We put the subject before the verb.
Is the teenager driving too fast? Will my teenage brother follow my advice?	The app can tell you **if the teenager is driving too fast**. I wonder **whether my teenage brother will follow my advice**.
Yes/No questions with auxiliaries or ***be***	We remove *do/does/did.* We add *if* or *whether.* The verb shows the -*s* ending for *he, she,* or *it,* in the present or the past form.
Does my teenager follow my advice? Did you do the same thing when you were my age?	I want to know **if my teenager follows my advice**. My son wants to know **whether I did the same thing when I was his age**.

An included question can be used after phrases such as these:

I don't know	I'm not sure	Do you remember
Please tell me	Nobody knows	Can you tell me
I have no idea	I can't understand	Do you understand
I wonder	I'd like to know	Would you like to know
I don't remember	I can't tell you	Does anyone know
You need to decide	It's important to ask	Do you know

[5] Grammar books often refer to included questions as "embedded questions."

continued

Language Notes:

1. We can add *or not* at the end of an included *yes/no* question.

   I'm not sure *if/whether* my teenage sister follows my advice **or not**.

2. We can add *or not* directly after *whether,* but not directly after *if.*

   I'm not sure **whether or not** my teenage sister follows my advice.

3. In an included question, sometimes the pronouns must be changed.

   How old were **you** when **you** started to drive?
   My daughter wants to know how old **I** was when **I** started to drive.

Punctuation Note:

We use a period at the end of the included question if the sentence is a statement. We use a question mark if the sentence begins with a question.

I don't know how fast she drives.
Do you know how fast she drives?

Usage Note:

When asking for information, an included question sounds more polite than a direct question.

Direct Question: Who took the car keys?
More Polite: Do you know who took the car keys?

EXERCISE 6 Fill in the blanks with *who, what, where, when, why, how, how many, how much, if,* or *whether.* In some cases, more than one answer is possible.

1. I don't know ___where___ my teenage son is.
2. Can you tell me ___if OR whether___ the app is useful or not?
3. I don't understand ______________ teenagers take so many risks.
4. Do you know ______________ I can buy the app online?
5. Do you know ______________ the app costs?
6. I don't know ______________ my teenage sister is a good driver or not.
7. Parents want to know ______________ they can do to keep their teenagers safe.
8. Do you know ______________ teenagers die in traffic accidents?
9. Professor Steinberg remembers ______________ kind of behavior he had as a teenager.
10. He studies ______________ the teenage brain works.
11. I wonder ______________ teenagers understand how risky their behavior is.
12. Do you know ______________ began the study of teenage brains? Was it Steinberg?
13. Do you know ______________ Steinberg does his study? At what university?
14. I don't know ______________ or not my cell phone has this app.

15. I'm fifteen years old. Can you tell me ________________ I'm old enough to get my driver's license?

EXERCISE 7 Write these questions as included questions after the words given. These are questions about the subject.

1. Who has an app to check their teenager's driving habits?

   I don't know who has an app to check their teenager's driving habits.

2. What happens if teenagers text while driving?

   Can you tell me ________________

3. How many teenagers are involved in accidents each year?

   I don't know ________________

4. Who invented this app?

   I wonder ________________

5. Which parents use this app?

   I'd like to know ________________

EXERCISE 8 Write these questions as included questions after the words given. These are *wh-* questions with *be* or an auxiliary verb.

1. When will your sister get her driver's license?

   I'd like to know when your sister will get her driver's license.

2. Why are teenagers so careless?

   Do you know ________________

3. Why are scientists studying the teenage brain?

   I'd like to know ________________

4. When can teenagers get their driver's license in this state?

   I don't know ________________

5. When is the brain fully developed?

   Scientists want to know ________________

EXERCISE 9 Write these questions as included questions after the words given. These are *wh-* questions with *do, does,* or *did.*

1. How do scientists study the brain?

   I wonder how scientists study the brain.

2. Why do teenagers take risks?

   I wonder ______________________________

3. When did you get your driver's license?

   Please tell me ______________________________

4. How do new technologies affect driving habits?

   It's interesting to know ______________________________

5. How does Professor Steinberg study the teenage brain?

   I'd like to know ______________________________

EXERCISE 10 Write these questions as included questions after the words given. These are *yes/no* questions with *do, does,* or *did.*

1. Do teenagers drive too fast?

   I'd like to know if teenagers drive too fast.

2. Do teenagers understand the risk?

   I wonder ______________________________

3. Does your son's cell phone have this app?

   Can you tell me ______________________________

4. Did you drive carefully when you were a teenager?

   Do you remember ______________________________

5. Does the brain develop completely by the age of twenty?

   I'm not sure ______________________________

EXERCISE 11 A mother is asking her teenage son some questions before giving him the car keys. Write these questions as included questions using the phrases given.

1. Where are you going?

   I want to know where you are going.

2. Why do you need to use the car?

You have to tell me ____

3. What time will you come back home?

Please tell me ____

4. Is there going to be another teenager in the car?

I'd like to know ____

5. How many kids are going to be in the car?

Please tell me ____

6. Does your friend have permission from his parents?

Do you know ____

7. Where does your friend live?

I don't know ____

8. Did I ever meet this friend?

I don't remember ____

10.3 Question Words Followed by an Infinitive

Some included questions can be shortened to an infinitive phrase.

Examples	Explanation
What should I do about my daughter? (a) I don't know **what I should do** about her. (b) I don't know **what to do** about her. How can I find a driving app? (a) Please tell me **how I can find one**. (b) Please tell me **how to find one**.	Some included *wh-* questions with *can, could,* and *should* can be shortened. Sentences (a) use a noun clause. Sentences (b) use an infinitive phrase.
Should I let my teenager use the car? (a) I can't decide **if I should let her use it**. (b) I can't decide **whether to let her use it**.	Some included *yes/no* questions can be shortened. Sentence (a) uses a noun clause. Sentence (b) uses an infinitive phrase. We use *whether,* not *if,* to introduce an infinitive phrase.

Language Notes:

An infinitive is commonly used after phrases such as these:

I don't know	I don't remember	I don't understand	Please tell me
I can't decide	I can show you	I forgot	I need to know

EXERCISE 12 Fill in the blanks with one of the words from the box below. You may use a verb more than once.

to compare	to chat	to get	to begin	to write	to make	to do

A: I need to go to my friend Marek's house. Mom won't let me use the car. I don't know how ___to get___ (1.) there without a car. Can you drive me there?

B: I'm busy studying for a test. Why do you have to go to his house?

A: We have to work on a project together. We can't decide what ______________ (2.).

B: What's your assignment?

A: We have to write about children in different countries. We can't decide what countries ______________ (3.). We don't even know where ______________ (4.).

B: Well, since we're from Russia, why don't you compare Russia with your friend's country?

A: He's from Poland. I'm not sure that our countries are so different.

B: I'm sure there are lots of differences.

A: We don't know whether ______________ (5.) about small children or teenagers.

B: Since you're a teenager, you know a lot about that subject already.

A: You're right. That's a good place to begin. But we don't know what kind of comparisons ______________ (6.).

B: You could compare education, number of children in a typical family, the kinds of games or electronics they have, or whether the family lets them use the car or not. There are a lot of things.

A: I'd really like to get together with my friend so we can brainstorm these ideas.

B: Why don't you just use a video chat?

A: I forgot how ______________ (7.) online. I haven't done it in a long time.

B: Don't worry. I'll show you what ______________ (8.).

A: Thanks!

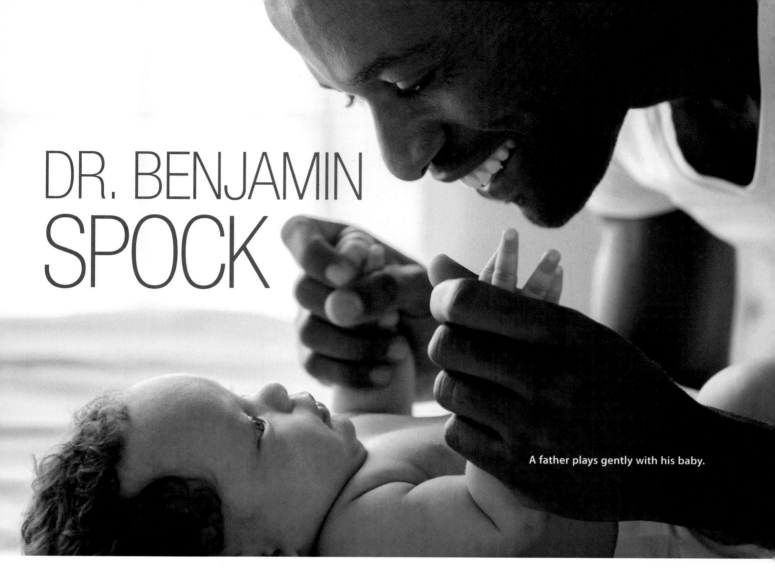

DR. BENJAMIN SPOCK

A father plays gently with his baby.

Read the following article. Pay special attention to the words in bold.

CD 2
TR 21

New parents worry that they might be making a mistake with their new baby. The baby cries, and they don't know if they should let him cry or pick him up. The baby is sick, and they don't know what to do. **"Trust yourself. You know more than you think you do,"** wrote Benjamin Spock in his famous book *Dr. Spock's Baby and Child Care,* which first appeared in 1946. This book has sold over 50 million copies, making it one of the biggest-selling books of all time. For many parents, this book is the parents' favorite guide for raising children.

Before Dr. Spock's book appeared, John Watson was the leading child-care expert in the 1920s and 1930s. He wrote, **"Never hug or kiss your children; never let them sit in your lap."** He continued, **"If you must, kiss them once on the forehead when they say good night. Shake hands with them in the morning."** Also, he told parents **that it was necessary to feed children on a rigid schedule.** Dr. Spock disagreed with this strict manner of raising children and decided **that he would write a book. "I wanted to be supportive of parents rather than scold[6] them,"** Dr. Spock said. **"Every baby needs to be smiled at, talked to, played with . . . gently and lovingly. Be natural and enjoy your baby."**

When Dr. Spock died in 1998 at the age of ninety-four, his book was in its seventh edition. He will be remembered for his common-sense advice. **"Respect children because they deserve respect, and they'll grow up to be better people."**

[6] *to scold:* to tell someone, in an angry way, that he or she did something wrong

COMPREHENSION CHECK Based on the reading, tell if the statement is true (**T**) or false (**F**).

1. Attitudes toward raising children have always been pretty much the same.
2. Dr. Spock had a gentle approach to taking care of babies.
3. People are still buying the 1946 edition of Dr. Spock's book.

10.4 Exact Quotes

Examples	Explanation
Dr. Spock said, **"Trust yourself."** John Watson said, **"Never hug or kiss your children."**	An exact quote is used when the exact words are worth repeating and are remembered because they have been recorded on video or audio or in print.
Dr. Spock said, "Every baby needs to be smiled at." "Every baby needs to be smiled at," **Dr. Spock said.** "Every baby needs to be smiled at," **said Dr. Spock.**	The *said* or *asked* clause can come at the beginning or the end of a quote. If it comes at the end, the subject and the verb can be inverted.
"More than anything else," **said Dr. Spock,** "children want to help. It makes them feel grown up."	An exact quote can be split, with the *said* or *asked* clause in the middle, separated from the quote by commas.

Punctuation Note:

Study the punctuation of sentences that contain an exact quote. Note that the first letter of an exact quote is a capital.

Dr. Spock said, "Trust yourself."
The mother asked, "Why is the baby crying?"
"Why is he crying?" asked the father.
"We need to feed him," said the mother.
"More than anything else," said Dr. Spock, "children want love."

EXERCISE 13 Read these quotes. Add capital letters, quotation marks, and other punctuation.

1. Watson said, ~~never~~ "Never hug or kiss your children."
2. Watson said give your children a pat on the head if they have made an extraordinarily good job of a difficult task
3. Dr. Spock said you know more than you think you do
4. I wanted to be supportive of parents said Dr. Spock
5. Parents can dramatically influence systems in their child's brain wrote child psychologist Margot Sunderland
6. To reduce violence in our society said Dr. Spock we must eliminate violence in the home and on television

7. Adolescence is a period of significant changes in brain structure and function wrote Dr. Steinberg

8. Parents sometimes ask what is wrong with teenagers why do they take so many risks

9. This process of maturation once thought to be largely finished by elementary school continues throughout adolescence wrote David Dobbs in a *National Geographic* article

10.5 Exact Quotes vs. Reported Speech

Exact quote	Reported speech
Dr. Spock said, **"You know more than you think you do."**	Dr. Spock told parents **that they knew more than they thought they did**.
John Watson said, **"It is necessary to feed children on a rigid schedule."**	John Watson told parents **that it was necessary to feed children on a rigid schedule**.
Dr. Steinberg wrote, **"I liked driving fast."**	Dr. Steinberg said **that he had liked driving fast**.

Language Notes:

1. We use an exact quote when we want to write exactly what someone has said. Exact quotes are common in stories and news reports.
2. We use reported speech when we want to report what someone has said.

EXERCISE 14 In the paragraph below, underline the noun clauses that show reported speech. Circle the verbs in the noun clauses.

Last week my daughter's teacher called me at work and told me that my daughter had a fever and was resting in the nurse's office. I told my boss that I needed to leave work immediately. He said that it would be fine. As I was driving my car on the highway to the school, a police officer stopped me. She said that I was driving too fast. She said that I had been going ten miles per hour over the limit. I told her that I was in a hurry because my daughter was sick. I said I needed to get to her school quickly. I told the police officer that I was sorry, that I hadn't realized I had been driving so fast. She said she wouldn't give me a ticket that time, but that I should be more careful in the future, whether my daughter was sick or not.

10.6 The Rule of Sequence of Tenses

After a past tense verb in the main clause (such as *said, told, reported, wrote,* etc.), the tense of the verb in the noun clause moves back one tense. This grammatical change is called the rule of sequence of tenses. Observe the difference in verb tenses in the exact quotes on the left and the reported speech on the right.

Exact quote	Reported speech
He said, "I **know** you." (present)	He said (that) he **knew** me. (simple past)
He said, "I **am studying**." (present continuous)	He said (that) he **was studying**. (past continuous)
He said, "She **saw** me yesterday." (simple past)	He said (that) she **had seen** him the day before. (past perfect)
He said, "She **was helping** me." (past continuous)	He said (that) she **had been helping** him. (past perfect continuous)
He said, "I **have taken** the test." (present perfect)	He said (that) he **had taken** the test. (past perfect)
He said, "I **had** never **done** that." (past perfect)	He said (that) he **had** never **done** that. *(No change)* (past perfect)
Modals	
He said, "I **can** help you tomorrow."	He said (that) he **could** help me the next day.
He said, "She **may** leave early." *(possibility)*	He said (that) she **might** leave early.
He said, "You **may** go." *(permission)*	He said (that) **I could** go.
He said, "I **must** go."	He said (that) he **had to** go.
He said, "I **will** stay."	He said (that) he **would** stay.
He said, "You **should** leave."	He said (that) **I should** leave. *(No change)*
He said, "You **must have** known."	He said (that) I **must have** known. *(No change)*

Language Notes:

1. Observe all the differences between a sentence that has an exact quote and a sentence that uses reported speech.

   Exact Quote:
   She said, **"I will help you tomorrow."**
   - quotation marks
   - comma after *said*
   - doesn't contain *that*
   - pronouns = *I, you*
   - verb = *will help*
   - time = *tomorrow*

   Reported Speech:
   She said *(that) she would* **help** *me the next day.*
   - no quotation marks
   - no comma after *said*
   - contains *that* (optional)
   - pronouns = *she, me*
   - verb = *would help*
   - time = *the next day*

2. Other time word changes in reported speech:

   today → that day
   yesterday → the day before; the previous day
   tomorrow → the next day; the following day
   this morning → that morning
   tonight → that night
   now → at that time

3. We even change the tense in the following sentence:

   The teacher asked me what my name **was**.

   Even though your name is still the same, the tense shows that the conversation took place at a different time and place.

EXERCISE 15 An adult is talking about things her parents and grandparents used to tell her when she was a little girl. Change to reported speech. Follow the rule of sequence of tenses.

1. You are the love of my life.

   My grandmother told me that I was the love of her life.

2. You will always be my baby.

   My mother said that I would always be her baby

3. You have an easy life compared to mine.

   My father told me that I had an easy life compared to his

4. We had a much harder life.

   My grandparents told me that they had had a much harder life

5. We want you to be happy.

   My parents said that they wanted me to be happy

6. You have to listen to your teacher.

   My father told me that I had to listen to my teache

7. You can be anything you want if you study hard. *(Change all three verbs.)*

   My parents told me that I could be anything I wanted if I studied hard

8. We don't want you to make poor choices.

   My parents told me that they didn't want me to make poor choices.

9. I was always a good student.

   My father said that he had been always a good student

10. We will always love you.

    My grandparents said that they would always love me

11. You should follow your dreams.

    My mother told me that I should follow your dreams

12. You can get your driver's license when you're sixteen. *(Change both verbs.)*

    My parents told me that I could get my driver's license when I was 16.

13. You should have studied harder.

    My parents said that ____________________

10.7 *Say* vs. *Tell*

Examples	Explanation
She **said that** her son was a good driver.	In reported speech, we ***say*** *that . . .* *Say* is not followed by an indirect object.
She **told me that** her son was a good driver.	In reported speech, we ***tell*** *someone that . . .* *Tell* is followed by an indirect object.
She **said,** "I love you." She **said to her daughter,** "I love you."	In an exact quote, we use *say* or *say to someone.* We do not usually use *tell* in an exact quote.

Language Notes:

1. Other verbs used in reported speech that do not have an indirect object are: *add, answer, explain, reply.*

   She **explained that** she had never had an accident.

2. Other verbs used in reported speech that have an indirect object are: *inform, notify, remind, promise.*

   She **reminded her son that** he should drive safely.

EXERCISE 16 Fill in the blanks with *said* or *told.*

1. He ___told___ his children that they should study hard.
2. I ___said___ that I was a very happy child.
3. I ___Said___ that I wanted to learn more about raising children.
4. Dr. Spock ___told___ parents that they should trust their instincts.
5. John Watson ___said___ that parents should not hug their children.
6. Dr. Spock ___said___, "You know more than you think you do."
7. The mother ___said___ to her son, "Eat your vegetables."
8. The mother ___told___ her son that she would pick him up after school.
9. My parents ___told___ me that they wanted me to get a good education.
10. I called my parents last week and ___told___ them about my new job.
11. The little girl ___Said___ to her mother, "I want to grow up to be just like you."
12. Our parents ___told___ us to be honest.

EXERCISE 17 Change each sentence to reported speech. Follow the rule of sequence of tenses.

1. Lisa said, "I need to put the kids to bed."

   Lisa said that she needed to put the kids to bed.

2. Lisa said to her son, "I'll read you a story."

   Lisa told her son that she would read him a story.

3. Lisa and Paul said, "We will take our kids to the park tomorrow."

   They said that they would take their kids the next day

4. Lisa said, "The children went to bed early last night."

   she said that the children had gone to bed early the

5. Lisa and Paul said, "Our son wants us to read him a story."

   they said thier son wanted then to

6. Lisa said to the teacher, "Our son's name is Tod."

   Lisa told her teacher that their son's name was

7. Tod said to his mother, "I don't want to go to bed."

   to her mother that he didn't want to go to bed

8. Tod said to his teacher, "I can write my name."

   Tod told his teacher he could .

9. Lisa said to Tod, "You must go to bed."

   Lisa told tod he had to go to bed

10. Tod said to his father, "I can't sleep."

    Tod told his father that he couldn't sleep

11. Paul said to Tod, "I don't want to argue with you."

    Paul told tod that

12. Paul said to Tod, "You should have studied harder for your math test."

13. Tod said to his friend, "My grandmother will buy me a toy."

continued

o his friend, "I love my new bicycle."

"I have never read Dr. Spock's books."

to his father, "I want to watch a program on TV."

xceptions to the Rule of Sequence of Tenses

	Exceptions to the rule
:nts **say** that Dr. Spock's book **is** their iide for raising children.	When the main verb is in the **present** tense, we do not change tenses.
told parents that children **need** love.	In reporting a general truth, it is not necessary to follow the rule of sequence of tenses.
:r has five children. He said that he **loves** He said that he **wants** to have more children.	In reporting something that is still true in the present, it is not necessary to follow the rule of sequence of tenses.
ıer said that she **will** (or **would**) pick up her class. rgarten teacher said that she **would** teach me shoes.	When a future action has not happened yet, we can use *will* or *would*. When the future reference is already past, we use *would*.
g kids isn't easy. t hear you. What did you say? that raising kids **isn't** easy.	When repeating speech immediately after it was said, we do not usually follow the rule of sequence of tenses.
other said that she **was** born in 1948. ıother said that she **had** (or **had had**) a childhood.	In reporting a statement about the past, it is not necessary to change the verbs if it is clear that the original verb was past. In sentence (a), it is clear that she said, "I **was** born in 1948." (It is rare to change *be* to past perfect if there is no confusion of time.) In sentence (b), it is clear that she said, "I **had** a difficult childhood."

18 Circle the correct verb to complete this essay. In some cases, both choices are circle both options.

'e two daughters. When I was a child, I said that I (*want/wanted*) to have a large family. But now
1.
an adult, I see how hard it is to be married, work, and raise kids. Before we were married, my
ı said that we (*will/would*) share child-care responsibilities. Yesterday it was his turn to take care of
2.

the kids. I told him that I (*need/needed*) [3.] some time to be with my friends and that we (*are/were*) [4.] going out to lunch. After I left, he told the kids that they (*can/could*) [5.] watch TV all day. I told him that our doctor always tells us that kids (*watch/watched*) [6.] too much TV. I told my husband that he (*needs/needed*) [7.] to take the kids out for exercise yesterday. But he told me that he (*wants/wanted*) [8.] to work on his car. He said that he (*will/would*) [9.] take them out next weekend. When I asked him about the lunch he gave the kids, he said that they (*ate/had eaten*) [10.] a lot of popcorn while they were watching TV so they weren't hungry for lunch. I always tell my husband that the kids (*shouldn't eat/shouldn't have eaten*) [11.] snacks before they eat a meal. Sometimes I say that I really (*have/had*) [12.] three children: my two kids and my husband!

10.9 Reporting an Imperative

Examples	Explanation
"Trust yourself." Dr. Spock **told** parents **to trust** themselves. "Read me a story, please." My daughter **asked** me **to read** her a story.	To report an imperative, an infinitive is used. We use *ask* for an invitation or request. We use *tell* for a command or instruction. We don't use *say* to report an imperative.
"Don't watch TV." My father told me **not to watch** TV.	For a negative, we put *not* before the infinitive.

EXERCISE 19 Change these imperatives to reported speech. Use *asked* or *told* + an object pronoun.

1. The mother told her kids, "Study for your test."

   The mother told her kids to study for their test.

2. The son said to his mother, "Give me a cookie, please."

   The son told his mother to Give him a cookie, Plea

3. She told the babysitter, "Don't let the kids watch TV all day."

   s " " " not to let the kids watch Tv all day

4. The girl said to her father, "Buy me a doll."

   she told her father to buy her a doll.

5. The mother said to her kids, "Eat your vegetables."

   The mother told her kids to eat their vegetables

continued

6. The father said to his daughter, "Help me in the garage."

The father told his daughter to help him

7. The girl said to her parents, "Take me to the zoo."

to take her

8. The dentist said to the boy, "Brush your teeth after every meal."

to brush her te

9. I said to my parents, "Don't spoil your grandchildren."

not to spoil

10. The girl said to her mother, "Comb my hair."

to comb her hair

11. The father said to his daughter, "Do your homework."

to do her h

12. The father said to his teenage daughter, "Don't come home late."

not to come home late

13. The father said to his teenage son, "Drive safely."

to drive safetly.

10.10 Using Reported Speech to Paraphrase

We often use reported speech when we want to paraphrase what someone has said. The exact words are not important or not remembered. The idea is more important than the exact words.

Exact quote	Reported speech
Dr. Spock said, **"You know more than you think you do."**	Dr. Spock told parents **that they knew enough to trust themselves**.
John Watson said, **"It is necessary to feed children on a rigid schedule."**	John Watson told parents **that they had to feed their children on a strict schedule**.
Dr. Steinberg wrote, **"Peer pressure declines as adolescents grow into adulthood."**	Dr. Steinberg said **that adults are not as influenced by their peers as teenagers**.

EXERCISE 20 Circle the correct words to complete this story. In some cases, both answers are possible, so circle both options.

Last month I babysat for a family that lives near me. It was my first babysitting job. They (*said/told*) that the children (*would/will*) sleep through the night and not cause any problems. But Danielle, the three-year-old girl, woke up at 9:00 and (*said/told*) that (*I/she*) (*can't/couldn't*) sleep. I (*said/told*) her that I (*will/would*) read (*her/you*) a story. Every time I finished the story, she (*said/told*) me (*read/to read*) (*her/me*) another one. She finally fell asleep at 10:00. Then Estelle, the five-year-old, started crying. When I went to her room, she told me that (*I/she*) (*has seen/had seen*) a monster in the closet. I tried to (*tell/say*) her that monsters (*don't/didn't*) exist, but she didn't stop crying. I tried to call the parents and tell them that Estelle (*is/was*) upset and that she (*is/was*) crying. They told me (*call/to call*) (*them/us*) in case of any problem, but when I called, there was no answer. Later they told me that they (*must/had to*) turn off their cell phone because they were at a concert.

1. 2. 3. 4. 5. 6. 7. 8. 9. 10. 11. 12. 13. 14. 15. 16. 17. 18. 19. 20.

They said (*we/they*) (*would/will*) be home by 11:00 p.m. But they didn't come home till 1:00 a.m. They called and told me that the concert (*has started/had started*) an hour late. I called my mother and told her that I (*couldn't/can't*) leave because the parents hadn't come home. She told me (*don't/not to*) worry. She said that it (*is/was*) my responsibility to stay with the kids until the parents came home. When they finally got home, they told me that (*we/ they*) (*don't/didn't*) have any money to pay (*me/you*) because they (*had forgotten/have forgotten*) to stop at an ATM. They said that (*they/we*) (*would/will*) pay (*you/me*) (*next/the following*) week.

21. 22. 23. 24. 25. 26. 27. 28. 29. 30. 31. 32. 33. 34.

When I got home, my mother was waiting up for me. I told her that I (*don't/didn't*) ever want to have children. She laughed and told me that the children's behavior (*wasn't/isn't*) unusual. She told me that (*you/I*) (*will/would*) change (*my/your*) mind someday. I (*said/told*) her that I (*didn't/don't*) want to babysit ever again. She told me that I (*will/would*) get used to it.

35. 36. 37. 38. 39. 40. 41. 42.

An Innovation in KIDS' TV

CD 2 TR 22

Read the following article. Pay special attention to the words in bold.

Joan Cooney and some of the Sesame Street characters at the 10th Sesame Street Workshop Benefit Gala

It is one of the most watched TV shows in the world. It is seen in 120 countries and is translated into a number of different languages. At the beginning, the producers were not sure if this program **was going** to be successful or not. They never imagined that more than forty-five years later it **would** still **be** here. Welcome to the world of Sesame Street.

In the 1960s, documentary television producer Joan Cooney realized that children **were watching** a lot of TV but **were learning** very little from it. Cooney wanted to investigate how television **could be used** to educate young children and entertain them at the same time. She thought that she **could help** prepare them better for school.

At first, TV producers didn't think that Sesame Street **would hold** the interest of young children. They thought that small children **didn't have** the attention span[7] to watch an hour of educational TV. Cooney thought otherwise. "What if it went down more like ice cream than spinach?"

Cooney brought in puppeteer[8] Jim Henson. Henson created the Muppets, with such characters as Big Bird and Elmo. Henson wanted to create characters that kids **could relate** to. Cooney realized that without these characters, learning the alphabet and learning to count **wouldn't be** as much fun.

The show was always excellent at helping kids learn the basics of numbers and letters, but it became clear that children's emotions **needed** to be addressed too. After the events of September 11, 2001, the producers realized that kids **had become** fearful and that they **needed** a way to express how they **were feeling**. So the show started dealing with children's fears. In 2002, the producers of the South African version of the program, "Takalani Sesame," thought that it **would** be a good idea to deal with HIV.[9] They understood how frightening this disease **could be** for small children, so they brought in a five-year-old Muppet named Kami, who is HIV positive.

It is clear that Sesame Street has evolved over the years. But it is still a favorite TV show for pre-school kids around the world.

---

7 *attention span:* the time that a person can concentrate on something

8 *puppeteer:* an artist who makes puppets behave like actors

9 *HIV:* human immunodeficiency virus

COMPREHENSION CHECK Based on the reading, tell if the statement is true (**T**) or false (**F**).

1. Children don't have the attention span to watch an hour of educational TV.
2. Not only does Sesame Street teach numbers and letters, it also deals with children's fears.
3. The characters in Sesame Street are the same in all countries.

10.11 Noun Clauses after Past-Tense Verbs

Examples	Explanation
The producers thought that small children **could learn** from TV. They didn't imagine that Sesame Street **would last** over forty-five years.	If the verb in the main clause is past (for example: *thought, realized*), we follow the rule of sequence of tenses in Chart 10.6.

EXERCISE 21 Use the words under the blank to complete each statement.

1. No one imagined that Sesame Street would be such a popular program.
   Sesame Street will be such a popular program.
2. Joan Cooney thought that ______
   Early education can be fun.
3. She realized that ______
   Small children are watching a lot of TV.
4. She thought that ______
   I can help kids prepare for school.
5. People believed that ______
   Kids don't have the attention span to watch a one-hour program.
6. The producers realized that ______
   Kids became fearful after September 11.
7. They thought that ______
   We should address kids' fears.
8. Parents were happy that ______
   Our kids can learn at home.
9. Dr. Spock decided that ______
   I will write a book about babies.
10. He thought that ______
    I can help parents feel more comfortable.
11. He knew that ______
    I want to help parents.
12. He told parents ______
    You can trust yourselves.
13. He never imagined that ______
    My book will become so popular.
14. I didn't know that ______
    I can use an app to check my son's driving habits.

10.12 Noun Clauses as Reported Questions

A noun clause can be used to report a question. If the main verb is in the past tense (*asked, wanted to know, tried to understand,* etc.), we follow the rule of sequence of tenses. (See Chart 10.8 for exceptions.)

Exact Quote	Reported Speech
Wh- **Questions with auxiliaries or *be***	
"How old are your kids?" "What are you watching on TV?"	She asked ***me*** **how old my kids were**. I wanted to know **what she was watching on TV**.
Wh- **Questions with *do/does/did***	
"How do kids learn?" "How did you get the idea for Sesame Street?"	She wanted to **know how kids learned**. Cooney was asked **how she had gotten (*or* got) the idea for Sesame Street**.
Wh- **Questions about the subject**	
"Which kids watched the show?" "Who saw the September 11 episode?"	She asked me **which kids (had) watched the show**. I wanted to know **who had seen (*or* saw) the September 11 episode**.
Yes/No **Questions with auxiliaries or *be***	
"Will young kids watch a one-hour program?" "Can kids learn the alphabet from TV?"	She wanted to know **if young kids would watch a one-hour program (or not)**. They asked her **whether (or not) kids could learn the alphabet from TV**.
Yes/No **Questions with *do/does/did***	
"Do small kids like Sesame Street?" "Did Jim Henson create the Muppets?"	She asked me **whether small kids liked (*or* like) Sesame Street**. I asked her **if Jim Henson (had) created the Muppets**.

Language Notes:

1. Remember: Reported speech is often a paraphrase of what someone has said.

   She asked me, "Do your kids spend a lot of time in front of the TV?"

   She asked me if **my kids watched a lot of TV.**

2. The most common changes that are made are:

   will → would　　　　can → could

EXERCISE 22 Change these exact questions to reported questions. Follow the rule of sequence of tenses. In some cases, it's not necessary to follow the rule of sequence of tenses.

1. Did you see the September 11 episode on Sesame Street?

   She asked me *if (or whether) I had seen the September 11 episode.*

2. How much TV do your kids watch?

   She asked me *How much tv my kids watched

3. Do they like Sesame Street?

She wanted to know ____

4. Why is this show so popular?

At first I didn't understand ____

5. Have you ever seen the show?

I asked my brother ____

6. How long has Sesame Street been on TV?

I wanted to know ____

7. Do you like Big Bird?

I asked my sister ____

8. Is Jim Henson still alive?

He asked me ____

9. How does Sesame Street handle scary situations?

We wanted to know ____

10. Has Sesame Street made any changes in the past forty-five years?

He asked me ____

11. Will the Muppets hold kids' attention?

Cooney wanted to know ____

12. Was Sesame Street the first educational TV program for kids?

I asked my teacher ____

13. How long will Sesame Street last?

They had no idea ____

EXERCISE 23 Choose the correct option to complete this essay. In some cases, both choices are possible, so circle both options.

When I was eighteen years old and living in my native Estonia, I didn't know where (*I wanted/did I want*)[1.] to go in my life. I couldn't decide (*I should/if I should*)[2.] get a job or go to college. I didn't even know what I (*want/wanted*)[3.] to study. Then I read an article about an *au pair* program in the U.S. This is a program where young people go to live with a family for a year to take care of their small children.

continued

I became very excited and asked my mother (*if I could/could I*) 4. apply. At first she said, "Absolutely not." She asked me why (*did I want/I wanted*) 5. to leave our family for a year. I told her that it (*will/would*) 6. be a good opportunity for me to improve my English and gain experience. My mother said she would talk it over with Dad, and they finally agreed to let me go.

After filling out the application, I had an interview. The interviewer asked me what kind of experience (*did I have/I had*) 7. with small children. I told her that I had two younger brothers and that I always helped my parents take care of them.

She also asked me (*whether/if*) 8. I (*knew/had known*) 9. how to drive. Sometimes an au pair has to drive kids to school and to play dates. I told her that I (*had/have*) 10. just gotten my license. I asked her how many hours a week I (*will/would*) 11. have to work, and she said forty-five. I wanted to know (*if I would/would I*) 12. get paid, and she said I would be paid about $200 a week. I also wanted to know (*if/whether*) 13. I (*would have/had had*) 14. the opportunity to go to school in the U.S., and she said yes. I asked her (*if or not/whether or not*) 15. I had to do housework, and she said that I only had to take care of the kids.

I was so happy when I was accepted. My year in the U.S. was wonderful. When I got back, I knew what I (*wanted/had wanted*) 16. to do. I majored in early childhood education and am now a pre-school teacher.

EXERCISE 24 Fill in the blanks to complete this story. Answers may vary.

I'm from Japan. I never imagined that I ___would be___ 1. in the U.S. someday. But I heard about an au pair program and decided to apply. I didn't know ______________ 2. my parents ______________ 3. me permission to come here, but they did. They thought that living in another country ______________ 4. me more independent and responsible. And they were right.

Before I came to the U.S. I wondered ______________ 5. my life ______________ 6. like. I thought that I ______________ 7. all the time and not have time for school and friends. But that's not true. I've made a lot of good friends in my English class. I didn't realize that I ______________ 8. people of different ages in a college class, but the students are as young as seventeen and as old as seventy-five! I was also surprised by how many people of different nationalities I ______________ 9.. I've met students from many countries, from Panama to Portugal to Peru! Before I came here, I thought that my English ______________ 10. almost perfect because I had been studying it since I was a child. But I realized that I ___________ (11.) a lot of expressions, like "It's a piece of cake" (it's easy).

I wondered ___________ (12.) the American family ___________ (13.) me. They treat me like a member of the family. I love their two pre-school kids.

At first I made one big mistake. One afternoon, when the parents were working, the kids asked me ___________ (14.) they ___________ (15.) watch TV. I thought that it ___________ (16.) OK. I let them watch whatever they wanted for as long as they wanted. I thought that I ___________ (17.) study while the kids were watching TV. When their mom came home, she was upset. She said that the kids ___________ (18.) allowed to watch only one program a day: Sesame Street. She thought that this program ___________ (19.) very educational and that other programs ___________ (20.) not so good for kids. She also told me that she ___________ (21.) the kids to use electronic devices a lot. She thought that it ___________ (22.) better for them to play with other kids than just play with electronics.

Little by little I'm learning about American family life and what parents expect from their kids.

EXERCISE 25 About You Fill in the blanks to talk about yourself and your parents when you were a child or a teenager. Follow the rule of sequence of tenses. Discuss your answers with a partner.

1. When I was a child, I dreamed that *I would be a movie star.*
2. When I was a child, I wondered *why everyone didn't speak the same language.*
3. My parents told me that ___________
4. My parents hoped that ___________
5. My parents thought that ___________
6. When I was a child, I thought that ___________
7. When I was a child, I didn't understand ___________
8. When I was a child, I never imagined ___________
9. When I was younger, I wondered ___________
10. When I was younger, I couldn't decide ___________

SUMMARY OF LESSON 10

Direct Statement or Question	Sentence with an Included Statement or Question	Explanation
She loves kids. She is patient.	I know **that she loves kids**. I'm sure **that she is patient**.	A noun clause is used as an included statement.
Is the baby sick? What does the baby need?	I don't know **if the baby is sick**. I'm not sure **what the baby needs**.	A noun clause is used as an included question.
What should I do with a crying baby? Where can I find a babysitter?	I don't know **what to do with a crying baby**. Can you tell me **where to find a babysitter**?	An infinitive can replace *should* or *can*.
You know more than you think you do. Do you have children?	Dr. Spock said, **"You know more than you think you do."** **"Do you have children?"** asked the doctor.	An exact quote is used to report what someone has said or asked.
Do your kids watch Sesame Street? I will teach my son to drive.	She asked me **if my kids watched** Sesame Street. She said **that she would teach her son to drive**.	A noun clause is used in reported speech after verbs such as *said, asked, knew,* etc.
Trust yourself. Don't give the baby candy.	He told us **to trust ourselves**. He told me **not to give the baby candy**.	An infinitive is used to report an imperative.

Punctuation with Noun Clauses	
I know where he lives.	Period at end. No comma before the noun clause.
Do you know where he lives?	Question mark at the end. No comma before the noun clause.
He said, "I like you."	Comma after *said*. Quotation marks around the quote. Period before the final quotation mark.
"I like you," he said.	Quotation marks around the quote. Comma before the final quotation mark. Period at end.
He asked, "What do you want?"	Comma after *asked*. Quotation marks around the quote. Question mark before the final quotation mark.
"What do you want?" he asked.	Quotation marks around the quote. Question mark before the end of quote. Period at the end.

TEST/REVIEW

Use the sentence under each blank to form a noun clause. Answers may vary.

Two years ago, when I was eighteen, I didn't know ___what to do___ (1. What should I do?) with my life. I had just graduated from high school, and I couldn't decide ______ (2. Should I go to college or not?). A neighbor of mine told me ______ (3. I had the same problem when I was your age.) and decided to go to the U.S. for a year to work as an au pair. She asked me ______ (4. Have you ever heard of this program?). I told her ______ (5. I haven't.). She told me ______ (6. I lived with an American family for a year.) and ______ (7. My English has improved a lot.). I asked her ______ (8. How much will this program cost me?). I was surprised to find out ______ (9. You'll earn about $200 a week.). I asked her ______ (10. Is the work very hard?), and she said ______ (11. It is.) but ______ (12. It is very rewarding.).

When I told my parents ______ (13. I am thinking about going to the U.S. for a year.), they told me ______ (14. Don't go.). They thought ______ (15. You are too young.) and ______ (16. You don't have any experience.). I reminded them ______ (17. I have babysat our neighbors' kids many times.). I didn't think ______ (18. Will they agree?), but to my surprise they did. When I filled out the application, I was afraid ______ (19. I won't be accepted.). But I was. My parents were worried. I told them ______ (20. Don't worry.). I promised them ______ (21. I will e-mail you almost every day.).

When I arrived, my American family explained to me ______ (22. What do I have to do?). They had two small kids, and I had to wake them, make them breakfast, and take them to school in the morning. I asked them ______ (23. Do I have to wait for them at school?). They told me that ______ (24. While the kids are in school, you can take ESL classes.). I told them ______ (25. I don't have enough money to pay for school.). They told me ______ (26. We will pay for your classes.). I was so happy to study English. When the year was over, I was very sad to leave my new family, but we promised ______ (27. We will stay in touch.).

Now I am back home and in college. My parents can see ______ (28. I've become more mature.) I don't know ______ (29. Is this experience for everyone?), but for me it was great.

WRITING

PART 1 Editing Advice

1. Use *that* or nothing to introduce an included statement. Don't use *what*.

   that
   I know ~~what~~ she is a good driver.

2. Use statement word order in an included question.

   he is
   I don't know how fast ~~is he~~ driving.

3. We *say* something. We *tell* someone something.

   told
   He ~~said~~ me that he wanted to go home.

   said
   He ~~told~~, "I want to go home."

4. Use *tell* or *ask*, not *say*, to report an imperative. Follow *tell* and *ask* with an object.

   told
   Dr. Spock ~~said~~ parents to trust themselves.

   me
   My son asked ^ to give him the car keys.

5. Don't use *to* after *tell*.

   She told ~~to~~ me that she wanted to be a teacher.

6. Use *if* or *whether* to introduce an included *yes/no* question. Use statement word order.

   whether
   I don't know ^ teenagers understand the risks while driving.

   if I should
   I can't decide ^ ~~should I~~ let my daughter get her driver's license.

7. Follow the rule of sequence of tenses when the main verb is in the past.

   would
   Last year my father said that he ~~will~~ teach me how to drive, but he didn't.

8. Don't use *so* before a noun clause.

   I think ~~so~~ raising children is the best job.

9. Use an infinitive to report an imperative.

   to
   My parents told me ^ drive carefully.

   not to
   My parents told me ^ ~~don't~~ text while driving.

PART 2 Editing Practice

Some of the shaded words and phrases have mistakes. Find the mistakes and correct them. If the shaded words are correct, write *C*.

When I was fourteen years old, I told my parents what (1.) I wanted to work as a babysitter, but they told me (2.) that (3.) I was too young. At that time, they told me that they will (4.) pay me $1 an hour to help with my little brother. A few times they asked me could I (5.) watch him when they went out. They always told me call (6.) them immediately in case of a problem. They told me don't (7.) watch TV or text my friends while I was working as a babysitter. They always told me that I have (8.) done a good job.

When I was fifteen, I got a few more responsibilities, like preparing small meals. They always told (9.) that (10.) I should teach my brother about good nutrition. I asked them whether I could (11.) get more money because I had more responsibilities, and they agreed. I asked them if I can (12.) buy something new with my earnings. My parents said (13.), "Of course."

When I turned eighteen, I started working for my neighbors, who have three children. The neighbors asked me had I gotten (14.) my driver's license yet. When I said (15.) yes, they were pleased because I could drive the kids to different places. I never realized how hard was it (16.) to take care of so many kids. As soon as we get in the car, they ask, "Are we there yet?" (17.) They think so (18.) we should arrive immediately. When they're thirsty, they ask me to buy (19.) them soda, but I tell (20.) them what (21.) it is healthier to drink water. They always tell (22.), "In our house we drink soda." I don't understand why do (23.) their parents give them soda instead of water. I didn't know whether to follow (24.) the rules of my house or theirs. So I asked my parents what should I (25.) do. My parents told me not to say (26.) anything about their parents' rules but that I should (27.) try to encourage healthy habits by example.

Little by little I'm learning how to take care of children. I hope that I will (28.) be as good a mom to my kids as my mom has been to me.

PART 3 Write About It

1. Write about some good advice your parents gave you when you were a child. Explain what the advice was and how this has helped you.
2. Write about how a teacher or another adult helped you or encouraged you when you were a child.

PART 4 Edit Your Writing

Reread the Summary of Lesson 10 and the editing advice. Edit your writing from Part 3.

LESSON

11 Unreal Conditionals Wishes

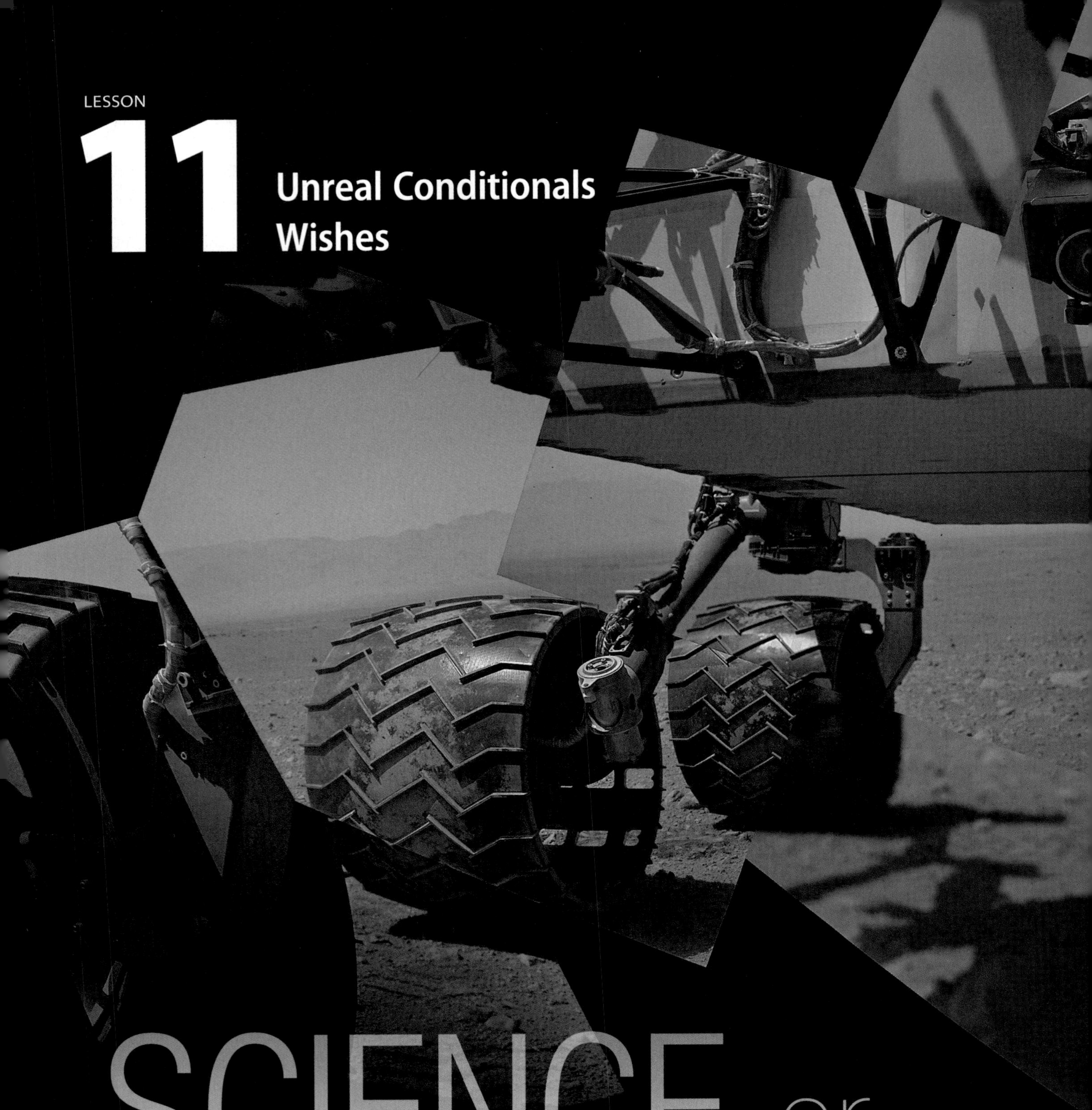

SCIENCE or SCIENCE FICTION?

Self-portrait taken by *Curiosity* rover on the surface of Mars

Somewhere, something incredible is waiting to be known.

—Carl Sagan

Time Travel

Wormhole

CD 2
TR 23

Read the following article. Pay special attention to the words in bold.

If you **could travel** to the past or the future, **would** you **do** it? If you **could travel** to the past, **would** you **want** to visit anyone? If you **could travel** to the future, **would** you **come** back to the present and warn people about possible disasters?

Time travel, first presented in a novel called *The Time Machine,* written by H.G. Wells over one hundred years ago, is the subject not only of fantasy but of serious scientific exploration.

About one hundred years ago, Albert Einstein proved that the universe has not three dimensions but four—three of space and one of time. He proved that time changes with motion. Einstein believed that, theoretically,[1] time travel is possible. The time on a clock in motion moves more slowly than the time on a stationary clock. If you **wanted** to visit the Earth in the future, you **would have to** get on a rocket ship going at almost the speed of light,[2] travel many light-years[3] away, turn around, and come back at that speed. While traveling, you **would age** more slowly.

Einstein came up with an example he called the "twin paradox." Suppose there is a set of 25-year-old twins, Nick and Rick. If Nick **decided** to travel fast and far on a rocket ship and Rick **decided** to stay at home, Nick **would be** younger than Rick when he returned. Specifically, if Nick **traveled** 25 light-years away and back, the trip **would take** 50 "Earth years." Rick **would be** 75 years old, but Nick **would be** 25 and a half years old. If Nick **had** a five-year-old daughter when he left, his daughter **would be** 55 years old. So Nick **would be visiting** the future.

Using today's technologies, time travel is still impossible. If you **wanted** to travel to the nearest star which is 4.3 light-years away, it **would take** eighty thousand years to arrive. (This assumes the speed of today's rockets, which is thirty-seven thousand miles per hour.) According to Einstein, you can't travel faster than the speed of light. While most physicists believe that travel to the future is possible, it is believed that travel to the past will never happen.

Although the idea of time travel seems the subject of science fiction, not science, many of today's discoveries and explorations, such as traveling to the moon, had their roots in science fiction novels and movies.

---

1 *theoretically:* possible in theory, but not proven

2 *speed of light:* 299,792,458 meters per second (or 186,000 miles per second)

3 *light-year:* the distance that light travels in a year through a vacuum (6 trillion miles or 9.46 trillion kilometers)

COMPREHENSION CHECK Based on the reading, tell if the statement is true (**T**) or false (**F**).

1. Scientists sometimes get ideas from science fiction.
2. Scientists believe that travel to the past is possible.
3. Einstein showed that time is dependent on motion.

11.1 Unreal Conditionals—Present

An unreal conditional is used to talk about a hypothetical or imagined situation. An unreal conditional in the present describes a situation that is not real now.

Examples	Explanation
If we **had** a time machine, we **could travel** to the future. (Reality: We **don't have** a time machine.) I **would visit** my ancestors if I **could travel** to the past. (Reality: I **can't travel** to the past.)	We use a past form in the *if* clause and *would* or *could* + base form in the main clause. When the *if* clause precedes the main clause, a comma is used to separate the two clauses. When the main clause precedes the *if* clause, a comma is not used.
If we **could travel** at the speed of light, we**'d be able** to go to the future.	All pronouns except *it* can contract with *would:* *I'd, you'd, he'd, she'd, we'd, they'd.*
If time travel **were** possible, some people **would do** it. If Einstein **were** here today, what **would** he **think** of today's world?	*Were* is the correct form in an unreal conditional clause for all subjects, singular and plural. However, we often use *was* with *I, he, she, it,* and singular nouns.
If I **were** in a time machine, I**'d be traveling** at the speed of light.	For a continuous time, we use *would* + *be* + verb *-ing*.
I wouldn't travel to the past **unless** I could return to the present. **Even if** I could know my future, I wouldn't want to know it.	A conditional can begin with *unless* or *even if.*
If I were you, I**'d study** more science.	We often give advice with the expression "*If I were you . . .*"
What if you **could travel** to the future? ***What if*** you **had** the brain of Einstein?	We use *what if* to propose a hypothetical situation.
If you **had** Einstein's brain, what **would** you **do**? If you **could fly** to another planet, where **would** you **go**?	When we make a question with conditionals, the *if* clause uses statement word order. The main clause uses question word order.

EXERCISE 1 Listen to the following sentences. Fill in the blanks with the words you hear.

CD 2
TR 24

1. If dinosaurs ___were___ (a.) alive today, the world ___would be___ (b.) very different.
2. Dinosaurs have been extinct for a long time. If dinosaur DNA[4] ________ (a.) not so old, scientists ________ (b.) possibly bring them back.
3. The world ________ (a.) unsafe for humans if scientists ________ (b.) back the dinosaurs.
4. Some people say that if scientists ________ (a.) back extinct species, the world ________ (b.) interesting and exciting.
5. Other people say that scientists ________ (a.) the natural order of things if they ________ (b.) back an extinct species.
6. What do you think? ________ (a.) a good thing if scientists ________ (b.) to bring back extinct species?

EXERCISE 2 Complete the conversation with the correct form of the verb given and any other words you see. Use *would* + base form in the main clause. Use the past in the *if* clause. Use contractions where possible.

A: If you ___could___ (1. can) clone any animal, which animal ________ (2. you/clone)?

B: I ________ (3. clone) my dog.

A: Why?

B: Well, my dog is getting old, and I don't want to lose her. If I ________ (4. can) make a copy of her, I ________ (5. have) the same dog again for many more years. What about you?

A: I just got a parrot, and they live about fifty years. I'm already forty years old. If I ________ (6. die) sooner rather than later, my parrot ________ (7. not/have) a home. Probably my parrot ________ (8. want) to clone me!

B: I read about cloning sheep, but I don't understand why scientists would do that.

A: I read something about it too. If you ________ (9. have) a cow that ________ (10. produce) high-quality milk or meat, it ________ (11. be) good business if you ________ (12. can) make many copies of this cow.

---

[4] *DNA:* molecules that carry the genetic information in living organisms

B: I hadn't thought about that. How about cloning people? If you ______________ (13. can) clone a good cow or sheep, why not clone a great person?

A: People have thought about cloning people. So far, it's never been done. Some people think that scientists ______________________ (14. *continuous form of* interfere) with nature.

B: But if you ______________ (15. can) clone a person, who ______________________ (16. you/clone)?

A: I think I ______________ (17. clone) Albert Einstein. I read that his brain is preserved. If scientists ______________ (18. take) the DNA from his brain, they ______________________ (19. be able to) make another Einstein.

B: What if the "new" Einstein ______________________ (20. not/ show) any interest in science? What if he ______________ (21. decide) to become a musician or a carpenter?

A: Hmm. I never thought of that. Also, the "new" Einstein ______________________ (22. *continuous form of* live) in a different world. He ______________ (23. have) access to computers and other new technologies.

B: And he ______________________ (24. not/have) the same parents or friends. If he ______________ (25. be) born today, I think he ______________ (26. be) a completely different person.

A: Well, it's fun to imagine.

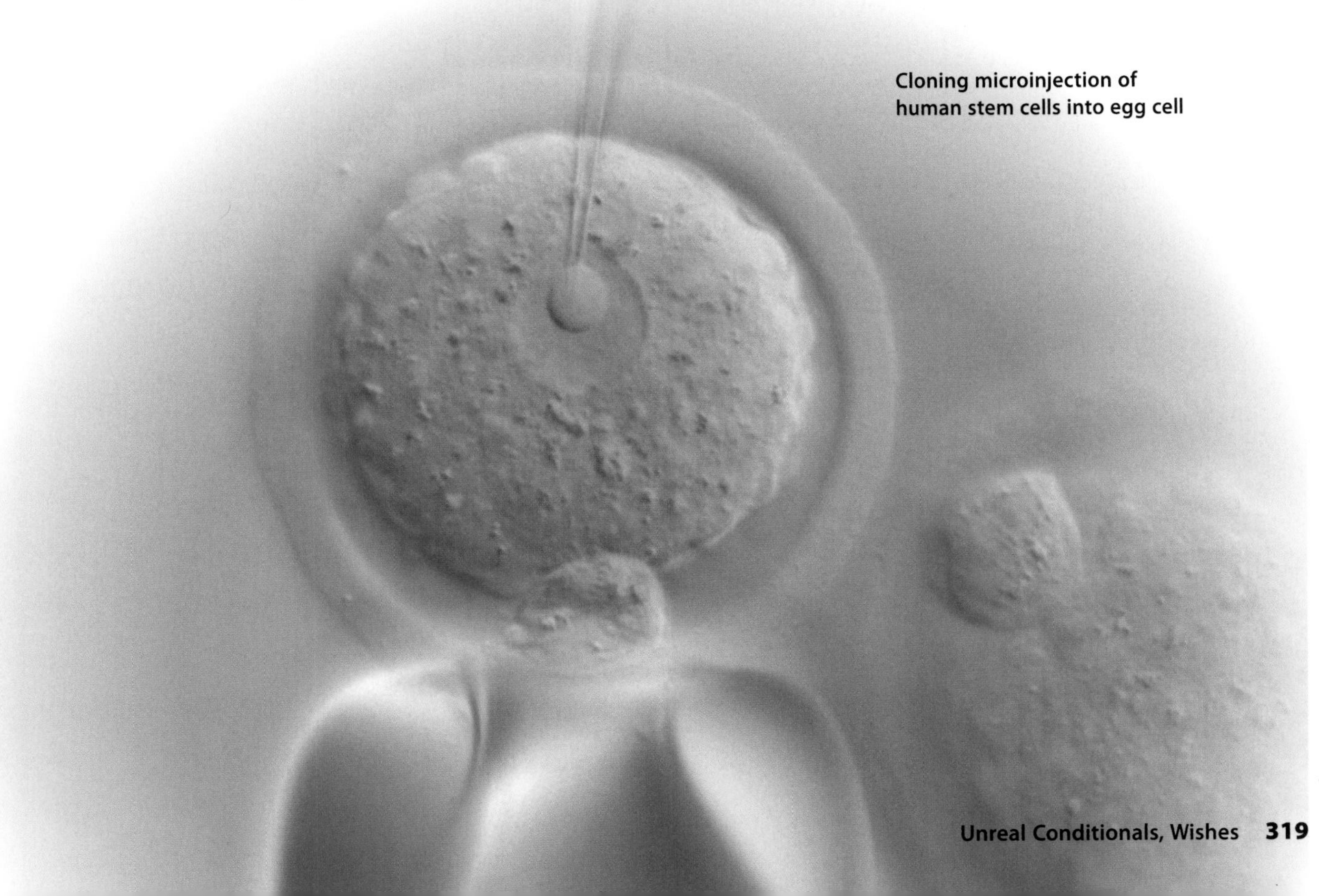

Cloning microinjection of human stem cells into egg cell

EXERCISE 3 Complete the conversations with the correct form of the verb given and any other words you see. Use *would* + base form in the main clause. Use the past in the *if* clause. Use contractions where possible.

1. **A:** What ___would you do___ (a. you/do) if you ___were___ (b. be) a scientist?

   B: If I __________ (c. be) a scientist, I __________ (d. try) to find a cure for diseases.

2. **A:** If you __________ (a. can) make a copy of yourself, __________ (b. you/do) it?

   B: My mom says that one of me is enough. If she __________ (c. have) two of me, it __________ (d. drive) her crazy.

3. **A:** If you __________ (a. can) come back to Earth in any form after you die, how __________ (b. you/come) back?

   B: I __________ (c. come) back as a dog. Dogs have such an easy life.

   A: Not all dogs.

   B: I __________ (d. only/come back) as a dog in a good home.

4. **A:** If you __________ (a. can) meet any person, dead or alive, who __________ (b. you/want) to meet?

   B: I __________ (c. want) to meet Abraham Lincoln.

5. **A:** If I __________ (a. can) find a way to teach a person a foreign language in a week, I __________ (b. make) a million dollars.

   B: You __________ (c. probably/make) a billion dollars. And I __________ (d. be) your first customer.

6. **A:** If you __________ (a. can) be invisible for a day, what __________ (b. you/do)?

   B: I __________ (c. go) to my teacher's house the day she writes the final exam.

7. **A:** What __________ (a. you/do) if you __________ (b. can/travel) to the past or future?

   B: I __________ (c. go) to the past.

   A: How far back __________ (d. you/go)?

   B: I __________ (e. go) back millions of years.

   A: Why?

   B: I __________ (f. be able to) see dinosaurs.

8. **A:** It ______ (a. be) nice if people ______ (b. can) live forever.

B: If people ______ (c. not/die), the world ______ (d. be) overpopulated. There ______ (e. not/be) enough resources for everybody.

A: I didn't think of that. If the world ______ (f. be) overpopulated, I ______ (g. never/find) a parking space!

EXERCISE 4 About You Answer the following questions. Discuss your answers with your partner.

1. If you could have the brain of another person, whose brain would you want?

   If I could have the brain of another person, I'd want Einstein's brain.

2. If you could travel to the past or the future, which direction would you go?

   ______

3. If you could make a clone of yourself, would you do it? Why or why not?

   ______

4. If you could travel to another planet, would you want to go?

   ______

5. If you could change one thing about today's world, what would it be?

   ______

6. If you could know the day of your death, would you want to know it?

   ______

7. If you could be a child again, what age would you be?

   ______

8. If you could change one thing about yourself, what would it be?

   ______

9. If you could meet any person from the past, who would it be?

   ______

10. If you could be any animal, what animal would you be?

    ______

EXERCISE 5 Fill in the blanks to tell what the following people are thinking. Use the correct unreal conditional and any other words you see.

1. One-year-old: If I ___could___ (a. can) walk, I ___would walk___ (b. walk) into the kitchen and take a cookie out of the cookie jar.
2. Two-year-old: If I ________ (a. can) talk, I ________ (b. tell) my mother that I hate peas.
3. Fourteen-year-old: I ________ (a. be) happier if I ________ (b. can) drive.
4. Sixteen-year-old: If I ________ (a. have) a car, my friends and I ________ (b. go) out every night.
5. Nineteen-year-old: I ________ (a. attend) a private university if I ________ (b. have) a lot of money.
6. Twenty-five-year-old: If I ________ (a. be) married, my parents ________ (b. not/worry) about me so much.
7. Thirty-five-year-old mother: I ________ (a. have) more time for myself if my kids ________ (b. be) older.
8. Sixty-year-old grandmother: If I ________ (a. not/have) grandchildren, my life ________ (b. not/be) so interesting.
9. Ninety-year-old: If I ________ (a. be) young today, I ________ (b. have to) learn all about computers and other high-tech devices.
10. One hundred-year-old: If I ________ (a. tell) you the story of my life, you ________ (b. not/believe) it.

EXERCISE 6 About You Give your opinion. Discuss your answers with a partner. Do you think the world would be better or worse if . . .

1. we could live to be 150 years old?
2. people didn't have to work?
3. every job paid the same salary?
4. there were no computers?
5. everyone spoke the same language?
6. we could predict the future?

11.2 Implied Conditionals

Examples	Explanation
I'**d** love to meet my great-grandparents. I **could** ask them about their lives. **Would** you **like** to see a living dinosaur? I **wouldn't want** to know the future. **Would** you?	Sometimes the conditional (the *if* clause) is implied, not stated. In the examples, the implication is "if you had the opportunity" or "if the possibility presented itself."

EXERCISE 7 Fill in the blanks with the missing words to complete the conversations. Use context clues. Use contractions where possible. Answers may vary.

1. **A:** ___Would___ (a.) you want to travel to the future?

   B: Not really. ________ (b.) you?

   A: Yes. It would ________ (c.) very interesting.

   B: I ________ (d.) happy.

   A: Why not?

   B: I ________ (e.) miss my family and friends.

   A: But you could come back and tell them about the future. You ________ (f.) them about future disasters.

   B: Then I ________ (g.) changing the future. And it takes a long time to come back. By the time I came back, everyone I know ________ (h.) much older.

2. **A:** I ________ (a.) love to know more about the past.

   B: Then you should study more history.

   A: But I wouldn't learn about my ancestors. I ________ (b.) only ________ (c.) about famous people.

3. **A:** ________ (a.) you want to live more than one hundred years?

   B: Yes. But I ________ (b.) to be healthy. What about you?

   A: I ________ (c.) want to see my great-great-grandchildren.

4. **A:** I ________ (a.) love to meet a famous person from the past.

   B: Who ________ (b.) you want to meet and why?

   A: Maybe Michelangelo. I ________ (c.) to watch him paint the Sistine Chapel.

5. **A:** ________ (a.) you ________ (b.) to see a living dinosaur?

   B: No, I ________ (c.).

   A: I think it ________ (d.) interesting.

   B: I ________ (e.) afraid.

6. **A:** I ________ (a.) to travel into space.

   B: I wouldn't want to. Why would you?

   A: I ________ (b.) what the Earth looks like from afar.

Mars, the Red Planet

EXPLORING MARS

CD 2
TR 25

Read the following article. Pay special attention to the words in bold.

Mars, our closest planetary neighbor, has always fascinated people on Earth. **If** you **watch** a lot of science fiction movies, you **see** people from Earth meeting strange-looking "Martians." But, of course, this is just fantasy.

In 2004, *Spirit* rover[5] landed on Mars to study the climate and geology of the planet, and to prepare for human exploration. In 2012, *Curiosity* rover landed on Mars. Its mission is to find out if there was ever life on that planet. One of the jobs of *Curiosity* is to figure out where a future mission should look for life. **If** enough information is gathered, astronauts **will** probably **arrive** on Mars by the 2030s.

Travel to Mars will be much more difficult than landing on the moon. When people landed on the moon, they carried with them all the supplies they needed. But sending a spaceship with people and all the supplies they need for their time on Mars would make the spaceship too heavy. So **if** astronauts **go** to Mars, scientists **will send** supplies first. Many other problems **will have to** be solved too.

Astronauts **will have** to return within a given time period. **If** they **don't come** back within this period of time, they **will miss** their chance of return. **If** astronauts **have** a problem with their equipment, they **will not be able** to rely on messages from Earth to help them. Because of the distance from Earth, it can take about forty minutes from the time a message goes out from Earth until it is received on Mars. Also, a visitor to Mars **will be** gone for at least three years because of the distance and time necessary to travel. But one of the biggest problems with traveling to Mars is the danger of radiation. Astronauts **will be** exposed to much more radiation than someone traveling to the moon.

If you **had** the chance to go to Mars, **would** you **go**?

---

[5] *rover:* a strong vehicle used for extraterrestrial exploration

COMPREHENSION CHECK Based on the reading, tell if the statement is true (**T**) or false (**F**).

1. Scientists are looking for signs of life on Mars.
2. One problem with traveling to Mars is exposure to radiation.
3. Astronauts on Mars will have quick communication with scientists on Earth.

11.3 Real Conditionals vs. Unreal Conditionals

Examples	Explanation
If astronauts **go** to Mars, they **will have** to return within a given time period. They **won't be able to** rely on scientists on Earth if they **have** a problem. **If** you're interested in Mars, you **should read** this article.	We can use *if* to describe a **real** future possibility. We use the present in the *if* clause and the future or a modal in the main clause.
If you **were** on Mars, you **would weigh** about one-third of what you weigh on Earth. If you **could** go to Mars, **would** you **go**?	We can use *if* to describe an **unreal** situation in the present. These examples are about hypothetical or imaginary situations. They are not plans for the future.

EXERCISE 8 Fill in the blanks with the correct form of the verb and other words given. Make real conditionals about the future. Use contractions where possible.

1. **A:** You're such a good science student.

   B: Thanks. If I ___get___ (a. get) a good grade point average in high school, I___'ll apply___ (b. apply) to the best universities. I want to major in chemistry.

2. **A:** I'm thinking about seeing the new science fiction movie this weekend.

   B: I love science fiction! If you ___go___ (a. go), I ___will go___ (b. go) with you. What day?

   A: I ___am going to go___ (c. go) on Saturday if I ___don't have to___ (d. not/have to) work that day.

3. **A:** I've just finished reading a great science fiction book. You can borrow it. But if you ___start___ (a. start) it, you ___won't be able to put___ (b. not/be able to put) it down. It's so good. Let me tell you about it.

   B: If you ___tell___ (c. tell) me about it, it ___will ruin___ (d. ruin) it for me. So please don't tell me.

4. **A:** I was going to rent the movie *Jurassic Park*. I heard it's about bringing back dinosaurs.

   B: I have it. I don't remember where it is, but if I ___find___ (a. find) it, you ___will be able to borrow___ (b. can/borrow) it.

   A: That's OK. My library has a lot of DVDs. If I ___look___ (c. look) in my library catalog, I ___will probably find___ (d. probably/find) it.

continued

5. **A:** I need to write a paper about cloning. I don't know much about it.

B: If you ______________ (a. google) "cloning," you ______________ (b. find) a lot of information.

A: If I ______________ (c. find) information about cloning humans, I ______________ (d. write) about that.

EXERCISE 9 Fill in the blanks with the correct form of the verb given. Use both real conditionals and unreal conditionals.

A: Do you think that astronauts will travel to Mars soon?

B: Not so soon. I read that there's too much radiation. If a person ______________ (1. be) exposed to too much radiation, it can be harmful. It could damage the bones or even cause cancer. Scientists are trying to build a spacecraft that can minimize radiation to the astronauts. If they ______________ (2. solve) the radiation problem, probably travel to Mars ______________ (3. happen) in our lifetime, possibly by the 2030s.

B: What about radiation at the airport security point? My cousin travels for business all the time. If she ______________ (4. pass) through radiation at the airport frequently, ______________ (5. she/get) cancer?

A: I don't think so. But if she ______________ (6. be) worried about it, she ______________ (7. can/ask) for a pat down. I love to travel. If I ______________ (8. can/go) anywhere, I ______________ (9. go) into space.

A: Me too. If I ______________ (10. go) to Mars today, I ______________ (11. bring) back a rock as a souvenir.

B: If you ______________ (12. leave) for Mars today, you ______________ (13. not/come) back for at least three years.

A: Oh. I ______________ (14. miss) my friends and family if I ______________ (15. can/not/see) them for three years. So maybe I'll take a more normal vacation. I'm thinking about going to Canada this summer. If I ______________ (16. go) there, I ______________ (17. visit) the Rocky Mountains.

B: If you ______________ (18. go), you can bring me back a souvenir rock from there. By the way, there's going to be a program on TV tonight about Mars. Are you going to watch it?

A: I don't know. If I ______________ (19. have) time, I ______________ (20. watch) it. If not, I ______________ (21. record) it.

LIFE One Hundred Years Ago

CD 2 TR 26 **Read the following article. Pay special attention to the words in bold.**

Most of us are amazed by the rapid pace of technology at the beginning of the twenty-first century. We often wonder what life will be like twenty or fifty or one hundred years from now. But do you ever wonder what your life **would have been** like if you **had been** alive one hundred years ago?

If you **had lived** around 1900 in the United States, you probably **wouldn't have graduated** from high school. Only six percent of Americans had a high school diploma at that time. If you **had been** a child living in a city, you **might have had** to work in a factory for twelve to sixteen hours a day, six days a week. In 1900, six percent of American workers were between the ages of ten and fifteen. If you **had worked** at a manufacturing job, you **would have had to work** about 53 hours a week and you **would have earned** about 20 cents an hour. (This is equivalent to about $5.00 an hour today.) Many of you **would have worked** on farms. Thirty-eight percent of laborers were farm workers.

If you **had been** a woman in 1900, you probably **wouldn't have been** part of the labor force. Only nineteen percent of women worked outside the home. If you **had gone** to a doctor, he probably **would not have had** a college education. And he **wouldn't have had** practical training before becoming a doctor. At that time, medical students learned only from textbooks.

If you **had had** a baby in 1900, it **would have been** born at home. If you **had gotten** an infection at that time, you **might have died**, because antibiotics had not yet been discovered. The leading causes of death at that time were pneumonia, influenza, and tuberculosis.

What about your home? If you **had been living** one hundred years ago, you probably **wouldn't have had** a bathtub or a telephone or electricity. You **would have been** living with a large number of people. Twenty percent of homes had seven or more people.

Do you think you **would have been** happy with life one hundred years ago?

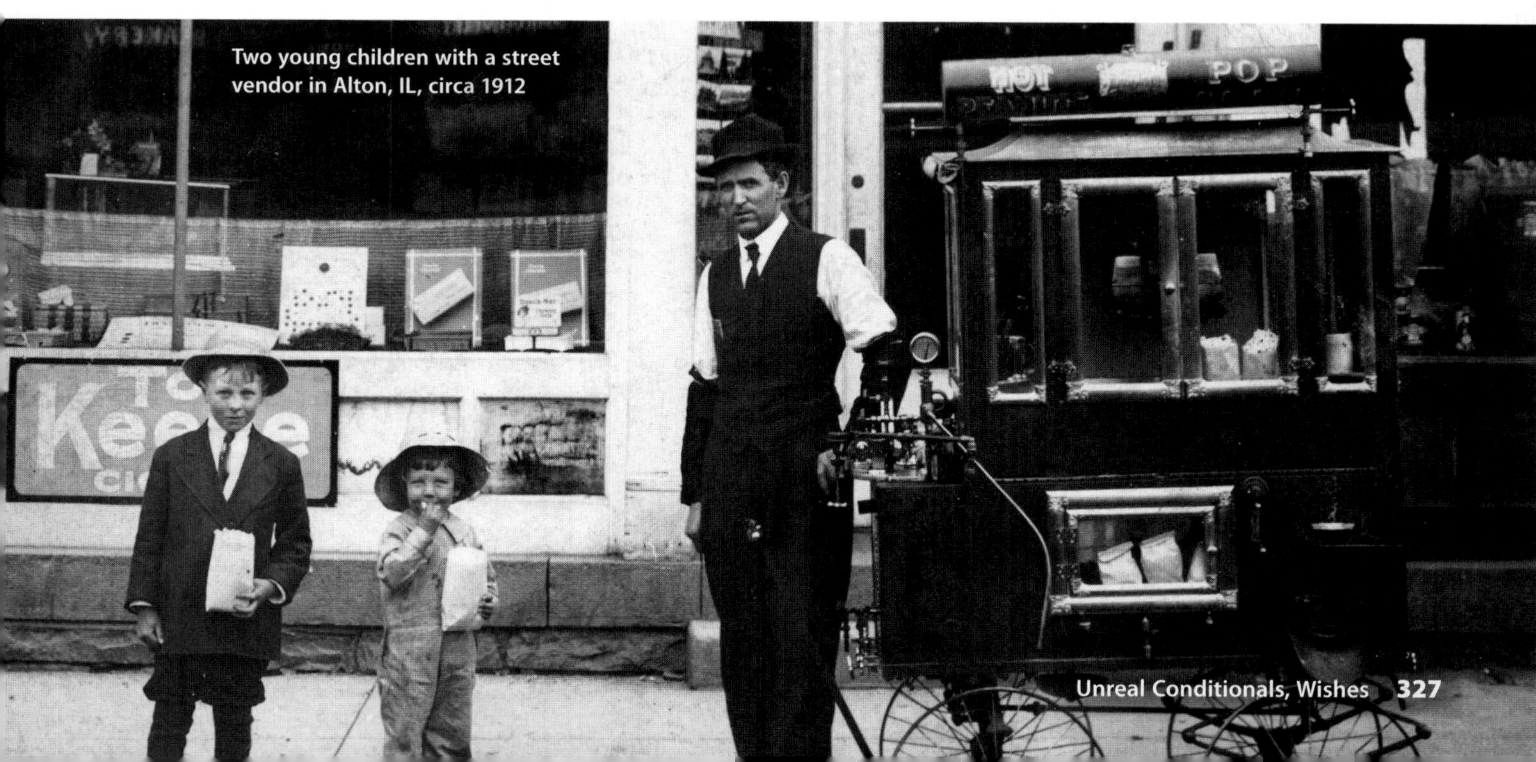

Two young children with a street vendor in Alton, IL, circa 1912

COMPREHENSION CHECK Based on the reading, tell if the statement is true (**T**) or false (**F**).

1. One hundred years ago, most children in the U.S. had to work. F
2. One hundred years ago, most doctors in the U.S. had a college education. F
3. One hundred years ago, most babies in the U.S. were born at home. T

11.4 Unreal Conditionals—Past

Examples	Explanation
If you **had lived** one hundred years ago, you probably **wouldn't have graduated** from high school. (Reality: You didn't live one hundred years ago.)	An unreal conditional can describe a situation that was not real in the past.
You probably **would have been** born at home if you **had lived** in the U.S. around 1900. If you **had gotten** an infection, you **might have died**.	We use the past perfect in the *if* clause and *would/could/might* + *have* + past participle in the main clause.
If my great-grandparents **had been able to** come to the U.S. one hundred years ago, I **would have been** born here and my life **would have been** different. (Reality: They couldn't come to the U.S. one hundred years ago.)	In the *if* clause, we use *had been able to* to express the past perfect of *could*.
(a) If you **were** born one hundred years ago, your life **would have been** different. OR (b) If you **had been** born one hundred years ago, your life **would have been** different.	Sometimes we don't use the past perfect, especially with the verb *be*, if it is clear that the action is past. It is clear that you *were* born in the past. Sentences (a) and (b) have the same meaning.

Language Notes:

1. In relaxed speech, *have* after *could, would,* or *might* is pronounced /ə/.
2. In very informal conversational English, we often hear *would have* in both clauses.

   If I **would have known** about the movie, I **would have told** you. (Informal)

   If I **had known** about the movie, **I would have told** you. (Formal)
3. Sometimes we mix a past conditional with a present result.

   If my mother **had** never **met** my father, I **wouldn't be** here today.
4. Sometimes we mix a present conditional with a past result.

   If I **were** an astronaut, I **would have gone to the moon**.
5. We can use a continuous tense with unreal conditionals.

   If you **had been living** one hundred years ago, you probably wouldn't have had a bathtub.

EXERCISE 10 Fill in the blanks with the correct form of the verb to complete this conversation about life in the U.S. one hundred years ago. Answers may vary.

1. If you ___had worked___ (a. work) in a factory, you ___would have earned___ (b. earn) about 20 cents an hour.
2. If you ___had had___ (a. have) a baby one hundred years ago, it probably ___would have been born___ (b. be/born) at home.

3. If you <u>had been</u> (a. be) a child in a big city, you <u>would have worked</u> (b. work) all day in a factory.

4. If you <u>had lived</u> (a. live) around 1900, you probably <u>wouldn't have finished</u> (b. not/finish) high school.

5. You <u>wouldn't have had</u> (a. not/have) a car if you <u>had lived</u> (b. live) at the beginning of the last century.

6. Your president <u>would have been</u> (a. be) Theodore Roosevelt if you <u>had lived</u> (b. live) in the U.S. at the beginning of the last century.

7. If you <u>had needed</u> (a. need) to travel to another city, you <u>would have traveled</u> (b. travel) by train.

EXERCISE 11 A middle-aged woman is telling her daughter how the young lady's life would have been different if she had grown up in the late 1950s. Fill in the blanks with the correct form of the verb given to complete the story.

It's great that you're thinking about becoming a doctor or astronaut. When I was your age, I didn't have the opportunities you have today. You can be anything you want, but if you <u>had been</u> (1. be) a woman growing up in the fifties, your opportunities ______ (2. be) limited. If you ______ (3. go) to college, you probably ______ (4. major) in nursing or education, or you ______ (5. take) a secretarial course. You probably ______ (6. get) married in your early twenties. If you ______ (7. get) pregnant, you probably ______ (8. quit) your job. You probably ______ (9. have) two or more children. Your husband ______ (10. work) to support you and the children. Also your house ______ (11. have) one TV and one phone. Because we had only one TV, the family spent more time together. You ______ (12. not/have) a computer or a cell phone. If you ______ (13. grow) up in the fifties, your life ______ (14. be) completely different.

EXERCISE 12 About You Complete each statement. Discuss your answers with a partner.

1. If I had been born 200 years ago, ______

2. If I had known ______, I ______

3. I wouldn't have learned about time travel if ______

The SCIENCE of AGING

Read the following article. Pay special attention to the words in bold.

CD 2 TR 27

Do you **wish** you **could live** to be one hundred years old or more? The answer to that question probably depends on how healthy you are at an advanced age, both physically and mentally. Does an elderly person **wish** she **had** the memory of a young person? Probably. As we age, the memory of most people diminishes.[6]

How much of longevity[7] and health is determined by genetics?[8] How much by environment? To analyze why some people live a much longer, healthier life than others, scientists have been traveling to areas of the world where there are a number of centenarians.[9] They have found certain groups in Japan, Italy, New York, and California who outlive others around them.

Women are more likely than men to live to be one hundred by a ratio of four or five to one. However, scientists no longer think that this is genetic. Women take better advantage of diet and medical care than men do.

For years, scientists **wished** they **could find** the genes for diseases. But now they have changed their focus. They are looking for genes that can protect us from disease and aging. Scientists are looking at the genes of the "wellderly" (well + elderly). These are people over eighty who have no chronic[10] diseases, such as high blood pressure or diabetes. They have found that, besides genetics, there are many factors that influence longevity—diet, education, response to stress, and even luck.

Salvatore Caruso, a centenarian from Italy, broke his leg when he was a young man. As a result, he was unfit to serve in the Italian Army when his entire unit was called up[11] during World War II. He **wished** he **could have served** with his unit.[12] "They were all sent to the Russian front,"[13] he said, "and not a single one of them came back." Whatever factors contribute to long life, a little luck doesn't hurt either.

6 *to diminish:* to lessen, reduce, or become limited
7 *longevity:* the length of life
8 *genetics:* the passing of physical characteristics from parents to children
9 *centenarian:* a person who is one hundred years old or older
10 *chronic:* long lasting, persistent
11 *to call up:* to ask someone to report for military service
12 *unit:* group of soldiers
13 *front:* the area where two enemy forces meet in battle

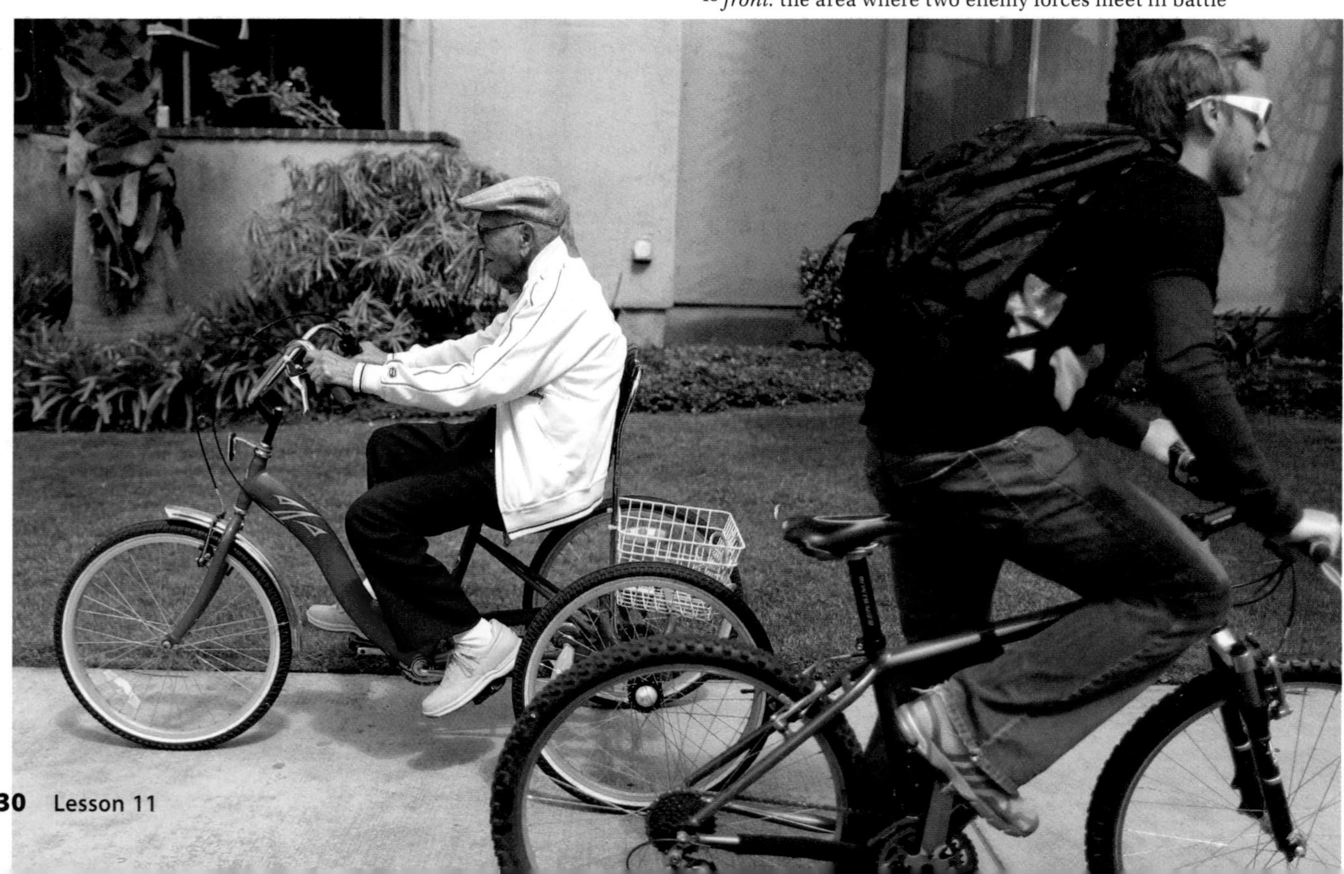

COMPREHENSION CHECK Based on the reading, tell if the statement is true (**T**) or false (**F**).

1. Some areas of the world have more centenarians than others. 
2. One factor that determines how long you will live is luck.
3. Salvatore Caruso was wounded in World War II.

11.5 Wishes

PART A

Examples	Explanation
Reality: We **have** to get old. **Wish:** I wish (that) we **didn't have** to get old. **Reality:** We **are learning** about Mars. **Wish:** I wish (that) we **were learning** about other planets too. **Reality:** I **can't live** 150 years. **Wish:** I wish (that) I **could live** 150 years.	We can wish that a present or future situation were different. We use a **past** verb for a wish about the **present or future**. After *wish*, we can use *that* to introduce the clause, but it is usually omitted.
I'm not young, but I wish (that) I **were**. I don't have a good memory, but I wish (that) I **did**.	We can use an auxiliary verb (*were, did, could,* etc.) to shorten the wish clause.
Reality: You don't want to study science. **Wish:** I wish (that) you **would study** more science. **Reality:** Scientists haven't found a cure for diabetes. **Wish:** I wish (that) scientists **would find** a cure for diabetes.	Putting *would* after a wish shows that one person wants a change in another person or situation. Using *would* sometimes conveys a complaint.

Language Note:

With *be*, the correct form is *were* for all subjects. In conversation, however, we often hear *was* with *I*, *he*, *she*, and *it*.

I wish I **were** younger. (Formal)
I wish I **was** younger. (Informal)

PART B

Examples	Explanation
Reality: I **didn't know** my grandparents. **Wish:** I wish (that) I **had known** them. **Reality:** Salvatore Caruso **couldn't serve** in the military. **Wish:** He wished (that) he **could have served**.	We can wish that a past situation were different. We use a past perfect verb for a wish about the past. If the real situation uses *could*, we use *could have* + past participle after *wish*.
I never knew my great-grandparents, but I wish I **had**.	We can use the auxiliary verb *had* to shorten the *wish* clause.

Usage Note:

In conversation, you sometimes hear *would have* + past participle for past wishes.

I wish I *would have known* my great-grandparents.

EXERCISE 13 Fill in the blanks to complete this conversation about present or future wishes. Use context clues to help you.

A: I wish we ___could stay___ (1.) young forever. Don't you?

B: I just read a book about how to extend your life.

A: Is it about some new scientific discovery?

B: Not at all. The authors are doctors. They write about things you can do to live a longer, healthier life.

A: Really? I wish I ____________ (2.) to be at least one hundred years old.

B: According to the book, there are a lot of things you could do to live longer.

A: Like what?

B: For one thing, the doctors recommend walking thirty minutes a day.

A: I wish I ____________ (3.) time for a thirty-minute walk. I work so many hours that I'm too tired to exercise when I get home.

B: Maybe you can walk to work.

A: No. I live too far. I wish I ____________ (4.) closer to my job.

B: How about walking on the weekend?

A: I have too many other things to do on the weekends, like laundry and shopping. I wish I ____________ (5.) so many things to do. When it's Monday and I start work, I wish it ____________ (6.) Friday. But when it's Friday and I have so many things to do on the weekend, sometimes I wish it ____________ (7.) Monday. What other advice does this book give?

B: The authors recommend that we sleep seven to eight hours a night.

A: I wish I ____________ (8.) so many hours, but I can't. I have too many things to do. It sounds like you have to work hard to live longer. There's no magic pill. I wish there ____________ (9.) a magic pill.

B: Me too.

EXERCISE 14 Fill in the blanks to show that one person wishes for something different in another person. Use *would* before the verb. Use contractions where possible.

1. (conversation between a grandfather and grandson)

   A: I wish I knew something about computers.

   B: Grandpa, you can still learn.

   A: I'm too old.

   B: I wish you __wouldn't say__ (a. not/say) that. You're never too old to learn.

   A: I wish you ____________ (b. teach) me.

   B: I promise I'll give you some lessons.

   A: You always say that. I wish you ____________ (c. not/make) a promise you can't keep.

2. (conversation between two friends)

   A: Let's go to the science museum on Saturday.

   B: I'd rather go to see a science fiction movie. There's a new movie I'd like to see. Let's go together.

   A: I wish you ____________ (do) what I want to do for a change.

3. (conversation between two cousins)

   A: I'd like to learn more about our ancestors.

   B: What for? Why focus on the past?

   A: I wish you ____________ (a. show) more interest in our family history. I'd love to know more about our great-grandpa. I wish you ____________ (b. send) your DNA to a genealogy site so that we can learn more about him.

   B: Why me? Why not you?

   A: Because I'm a woman. The DNA of a male gives more information about other males.

4. (conversation between two friends)

   A: I wish scientists ____________ (a. find) a cure for AIDS already.

   B: Me too. So many people have died of this disease. And I wish they ____________ (b. cure) cancer and other diseases too.

continued

5. (conversation between a wife and husband)

A: I wish you ______________ (a. take) better care of yourself. You never go to the doctor.

B: I'm not sick.

A: I wish you ______________ (b. get) a checkup every year.

EXERCISE 15 About You Fill in the blanks to complete each statement. Discuss your answers with a partner.

1. I wish I were ______________
2. I wish I knew how to ______________
3. I wish I didn't have to ______________
4. I wish I had ______________
5. I wish I could ______________
6. My parents wish(ed) I would ______________
7. I wish *(the name of another person)* would ______________
8. I wish the teacher would ______________

EXERCISE 16 Fill in the blanks for a past wish.

1. When my dog died, I really missed him. I wish I ___had cloned___ (clone) him before he died.
2. I didn't pay much attention to science when I was younger. I wish I ______________ (pay) more attention in my science class.
3. I'm so interested in dinosaurs. I wish they ______________ (not/become) extinct.
4. I used to have pictures of my great-grandparents, but I left them in my country. I wish I ______________ (bring) them here with me.
5. I wish I ______________ (live) in the 1800s, during the time of President Lincoln.
6. My grandfather died before I was born. I wish I ______________ (can/know) him.
7. I never asked my grandparents much about their lives. I wish I ______________ (ask) them more about their childhood before they died.

EXERCISE 17 About You Work with a partner and talk about something . . .

1. you wish you had done when you were younger.
2. you wish you had studied when you were younger.
3. your family wishes you had done differently.
4. you wish you had known before you came to this country.
5. you wish your parents had done or told you.
6. you wish had never happened.

EXERCISE 18 Fill in the blanks with the correct form of the verb given in each of the conversations. Some wishes are about the present; some are about the past. Some are wishes for a change.

1. **A:** I wish I ___had___ (a. have) good vision.

   B: Why don't you try laser surgery? I had it two years ago, and I don't need glasses anymore. I had worn glasses since I was a child. I wish they ______ (b. have) this surgery years ago.

2. **A:** I wish I ______ (a. be) thin.

   B: Why don't you try a diet?

   A: I've tried every diet. Nothing works.

   B: You need to exercise every day.

   A: I'm too tired when I get home from work. I wish scientists ______ (b. find) a pill that would make me thin with no effort on my part.

3. **A:** I've been bald since I was twenty-five years old. I wish I ______ (a. not/be) bald.

   B: They say bald men are very manly.

   A: I don't care what they say. I wish I ______ (b. have) hair. I wish someone ______ (c. find) a solution for baldness.

4. **A:** I wish I ______ (a. be) older.

   B: Why? No one wants to get old.

   A: I didn't say "old." I just said "older." Older people have more experience and wisdom.

   B: I wish we ______ (b. have) the wisdom of old people and the bodies of young people.

continued

5. **A:** I wish I ______________ travel to the future.
a. can

B: Why?

A: I would be able to see future problems and then come back and warn people about them.

B: I wish I ______________ go to the past.
b. can

A: Why?

B: I would want to meet my grandparents. I never knew them. I wish I ______________ them, but
c. know
they died before I was born.

6. **A:** We saw a great movie last night about time travel. Too bad you didn't come with us.

B: I wish I ______________ with you, but I had to study for my biology test.
can/go

7. **A:** I'm an only child. I wish I ______________ a sister or brother.
a. have

B: Maybe you will someday.

A: I don't think so. My parents are in their fifties. I wish they ______________ another child when
b. have
they were young.

8. **A:** We went to see a great movie last night. I wish you ______________ with us.
a. come

B: You didn't tell me about it. I wish you ______________ me. What was it about?
b. tell

A: It was about a man who wishes he ______________ rich. And his wish comes true.
c. be
He's suddenly very rich, and he starts to have all kinds of problems.

B: I wish I ______________ those kinds of problems!
d. have

EXERCISE 19 A mother (A) is complaining to her adult son (B). Fill in the blanks with the correct form of the words given to express their wishes. Some wishes are about the present; some are about the past. Some are wishes for a change.

A: You never visit. I wish you ___would visit___ me more often. I'm not going to live forever, you know.
1. visit

B: I do visit you often. Isn't once a week often enough?

A: Some day I won't be here, and you'll say to yourself, "I wish I ______________ my mom more often."
2. visit

B: Mom, you're only forty-eight years old.

A: Who knows how long I'll be here? There are no guarantees in life. My own mother died when I was a teenager. I wish she ______________ to see you and your sister.
3. live

B: I do too. But what can we do?

A: I wish you _______________ married already.
4. be

B: Mom, I'm only twenty-five years old. There's plenty of time to get married.

A: Well, your sister's only twenty-three, and she's already married. I wish you _______________
5. be
more like your sister. She finished college and then got married.

B: I wish you _______________ comparing me to my sister. She has different goals in life.
6. stop
Besides, you don't like her husband.

A: You're right. I wish she _______________ a different man.
7. marry

B: There's nothing wrong with Paul. He's a good husband to her.

A: We'll see. You know, you're too thin. I wish you _______________ more.
8. eat

B: I eat enough. When I was a teenager, you said I was too fat.

A: I'm still your mother. I wish you _______________ to me.
9. listen

B: I do listen to you. But I've got to live my own life.

A: Sometimes you act like a child and tell me you're old enough to make your own decisions. Then you tell me you're too young to get married.

B: I'm not too young to get married. I just don't want to do it now. I'm happy being a rock musician.

A: I wish you _______________ a real job.
10. have

B: I have a real job.

A: You didn't finish college. You left after your junior year. I wish you _______________
11. get
your degree.

B: You don't need a college degree to be a rock musician.

A: Well, I hope I live long enough to see you married, with a good job.

B: With today's technologies, you'll probably live to be 150 years old. I'll be 127, and you'll probably still be telling me how to live my life.

SUMMARY OF LESSON 11

1. Unreal Conditionals—Present

Verb → Past	Verb → *Would/Could/Might* + Base Form
If I **were** an astronaut,	I **would go** to Mars.
If I **could** live to be 150 years old,	I **would know** my great-great-grandchildren.
If you **could** travel to the past,	you **could meet** your ancestors.
If we **didn't have** advanced technology,	we **wouldn't be** able to explore space.
If you **took** better care of yourself,	you **might live** to be one hundred years old.

2. Unreal Conditionals—Past

Verb → Past Perfect	Verb → *Would/Could/Might* + *Have* + Past Participle
If you **had lived** one hundred years ago,	you **wouldn't have had** a computer.
If you **had been** a doctor one hundred years ago,	you **could have practiced** medicine without a college degree.
If my father **had** not **met** my mother,	I **wouldn't have been** born.
If you **had gotten** an infection one hundred years ago,	you **might have died**.

3. Real Possibilities—Future

Conditional	Result
If we **explore** Mars,	we **will learn** a lot.
If you **eat** a healthy diet,	you**'ll live** longer.

4. Wishes

Examples	Explanation
I wish my grandparents **were** here. I wish I **could go** to Mars. I wish we **were learning** about dinosaurs.	Wish about the present
I wish I **could live to be** one hundred.	Wish about the future
I wish my grandpa **would tell** me more about his childhood. My mother wishes my father **would take** better care of his health.	Wish for a change in another person or situation
I wish I **had studied** more science when I was younger.	Wish about the past

TEST/REVIEW

Circle the letter of the correct word(s) to fill in the blanks.

1. I ____________ help you with your science project if I had more time.

a. were　　c. would (circled)

b. will　　d. would be

2. I might become a scientist. If I ____________ one, I'll try to find a cure for diseases.

a. will become　　c. would become

b. became　　d. become

3. If I ____________ you, I'd spend more time on science and less on science fiction.

a. were　　c. will be

b. am　　d. would be

4. I can't help you with your project. I would help you if I ____________.

a. can　　c. would

b. could　　d. had

5. We can't travel at the speed of light. If we could travel at the speed of light, we ____________ able to visit far away stars.

a. would be　　c. would have been

b. will be　　d. were

6. We would know more about Mars if it ____________ so far away.

a. weren't　　c. wouldn't have been

b. won't be　　d. wouldn't be

7. Some people don't take good care of their health. If they ____________ better care of their health, they would probably live longer.

a. take　　c. had taken

b. would take　　d. took

8. I wouldn't go to Mars even if you ____________ me a million dollars.

a. pay　　c. will pay

b. paid　　d. would pay

continued

9. If I could visit any planet, I ________________ Jupiter.

a. will visit
c. would be visit
b. would visit
d. would have visited

10. I don't know much about science. I wish I ________________ more about it.

a. knew
c. have known
b. will know
d. know

11. We can't travel to the past. I wish we ________________ travel to the past.

a. could
c. can
b. would
d. will

12. If I had known my great-grandparents, I ________________ them about their childhood.

a. would ask
c. could ask
b. will ask
d. would have asked

13. My uncle never exercised and was overweight. He had a heart attack and died when he was fifty years old. If he ________________ better care of himself, he might have lived much longer.

a. would take
c. took
b. had taken
d. will take

14. Salvatore Caruso broke his leg and couldn't serve in World War II. If he ________________ in World War II, he might have been killed.

a. were served
c. would serve
b. has served
d. had served

15. My favorite dog died ten years ago. I wish I ________________ her.

a. clone
c. had cloned
b. will clone
d. would clone

16. I wish scientists ________________ a cure for AIDS.

a. find
c. would find
b. found
d. will find

17. I didn't study physics in high school, but I wish I ________________.

a. have   c. were

b. had   d. would

18. I don't know much about dinosaurs, but I wish I ________________.

a. had   c. would

b. were   d. did

19. If you ________________ the movie *Jurassic Park*, you would have been very scared.

a. had seen   c. would have seen

b. would see   d. will see

20. If scientists brought back dinosaurs back from extinction today, the world ________________ very dangerous for humans.

a. will be   c. would be

b. would have been   d. were

WRITING

PART 1 Editing Advice

1. Don't use *will* with an unreal conditional.

   If I ~~will be~~ were on Mars, I would look for life forms.

2. Always use the base form after a modal.

   The teacher would ~~has~~ have helped you with your science project if you had asked her.

3. Use the past perfect, not the present perfect, for unreal conditionals and wishes.

   If you ~~have~~ had seen the movie, you would have understood more about dinosaurs.

   I wish you ~~have~~ had seen the movie.

4. For a real conditional about the future, use the simple present in the *if* clause.

   If I ~~will~~ have time tomorrow, I will help you with your science project.

5. In formal writing, use *were*, not *was*, in an unreal conditional.

   I wish I ~~was~~ were a better student in science.

PART 2 Editing Practice

Some of the shaded words and phrases have mistakes. Find the mistakes and correct them. If the shaded words are correct, write *C*.

There are a few things in my life that I wish were (1. C) different. First, I wish I ~~have~~ had (2.) a better job and made (3.) more money. Unfortunately, I don't have the skills for a better job. When I was in high school, I wasn't interested in college. My parents always said, "We wish you would continued (4.) your education," but I was foolish and didn't listen to them. If I have (5.) gone to college, I will (6.) be making much more money now. And if I had (7.) more money, I could (8.) help my family back home. And, if I will be (9.) better educated, my parents would (10.) be very proud of me. I wish I can (11.) convince my younger brothers and sister about the importance of an education, but they'll have to make their own decisions.

Another thing I'm not happy about is my living situation. I have a roommate because I can't afford to pay the rent alone. I wish I don't have (12.) a roommate. My roommate always watches TV, and the TV is too loud. I wish he would (13.) turn off the TV at night and let me sleep. My parents have told me, "If I were (14.) you, I will (15.) get a better roommate." But we signed a one-year lease together and I can't do anything about it until next May. If I had known (16.) that he was going to be so inconsiderate, I never would had (17.) roomed with him. I wish it was (18.) May already! I prefer to live alone rather than live with a stranger. I'm saving my money now. If I will have (19.) enough money, I'll get my own apartment next May. Another possibility is to room with my cousin, who's planning to come here soon. If he comes (20.) to the U.S. by May, I share (21.) an apartment with him. He's very responsible. I wish he has come (22.) to the U.S. with me last year, but he didn't get his visa at that time.

I realize that we all make mistakes in life, but we learn from them. If I could (23.) give advice to every young person in the world, I'd (24.) say, "Look before you leap." And I will say (25.), "Listen to your parents. They've lived longer than you, and you can learn from their experience."

PART 3 Write About It

1. What do you think would be the advantages or disadvantages of cloning human beings?
2. Write about an important decision you made in the past. What would your life be like if you hadn't made this decision?

PART 4 Edit Your Writing

Reread the Summary of Lesson 11 and the editing advice. Edit your writing from Part 3.

APPENDIX A

Vowel and Consonant Pronunciation Charts

Vowels

Symbol	Examples
ʌ	l**o**ve, c**u**p
a	f**a**ther, b**o**x
æ	cl**a**ss, bl**a**ck
ə	**a**lone, at**o**m
ɛ	**e**ver, w**e**ll
i	**ea**t, f**ee**t
ɪ	m**i**ss, b**i**t
ɔ	t**a**lk, c**o**rn
ʊ	w**ou**ld, b**oo**k
oʊ	c**o**ne, b**oa**t
u	t**oo**th, thr**ough**
eɪ	**a**ble, d**ay**
aɪ	m**i**ne, tr**y**
aʊ	ab**ou**t, c**ow**
ɔɪ	j**oi**n, b**oy**

Consonants

Symbol	Examples
b	**b**read, ca**b**
d	**d**oor, **d**u**d**e
f	**f**orm, i**f**
g	**g**o, fla**g**
h	**h**ello, be**h**ind
j	**u**se, **y**ellow
k	**c**oo**k**, hi**k**e
l	**l**eg, **l**itt**le**
m	**m**onth, ti**m**e
n	**n**ever, **n**i**n**e
ŋ	si**ng**er, walki**ng**
p	**p**ut, ma**p**
r	**r**ive**r**, t**r**y
s	**s**aw, park**s**
ʃ	**sh**ow, ac**ti**on
ɾ	a**t**om, la**d**y
t	**t**ake, **t**en**t**
tʃ	**ch**eck, **ch**ur**ch**
θ	**th**ing, bo**th**
ð	**th**e, ei**th**er
v	**v**oice, o**f**
w	**w**ould, re**w**ard
z	**z**oo, ma**z**es
ʒ	u**s**ual, vi**s**ion
dʒ	**j**ust, e**dge**

Noncount Nouns

There are several types of noncount nouns.

Group A: Nouns that have no distinct, separate parts. We look at the whole.			
milk	yogurt	paper	cholesterol
oil	poultry	rain	blood
water	bread	air	
coffee	meat	electricity	
tea	soup	lightning	
juice	butter	thunder	

Group B: Nouns that have parts that are too small or insignificant to count.			
rice	hair	sand	
sugar	popcorn	corn	
salt	snow	grass	

Group C: Nouns that are classes or categories of things. The members of the category are not the same.	
money or cash (nickels, dimes, dollars)	mail (letters, packages, postcards, flyers)
furniture (chairs, tables, beds)	homework (compositions, exercises, readings)
clothing (sweaters, pants, dresses)	jewelry (necklaces, bracelets, rings)

Group D: Nouns that are abstractions.					
love	happiness	nutrition	patience	work	nature
truth	education	intelligence	poverty	health	help
beauty	advice	unemployment	music	fun	energy
luck/fortune	knowledge	pollution	art	information	friendship

Group E: Subjects of study.		
history	grammar	biology
chemistry	geometry	math (mathematics*)

***Note:** Even though *mathematics* ends with *s*, it is not plural.

continued

Notice the quantity words used with count and noncount nouns.

Singular Count	Plural Count	Noncount
a tomato	tomatoes	coffee
one tomato	**two** tomatoes	**two cups of** coffee
	some tomatoes	**some** coffee
no tomato	**no** tomatoes	**no** coffee
	any tomatoes (with questions and negatives)	**any** coffee (with questions and negatives)
	a lot of tomatoes	**a lot of** coffee
	many tomatoes	**much** coffee (with questions and negatives)
	a few tomatoes	**a little** coffee
	several tomatoes	**several** cups of coffee
	How many tomatoes?	**How much** coffee?

The following words can be used as either count nouns or noncount nouns. However, the meaning changes according to the way the nouns are used.

Count	Noncount
Oranges and grapefruit are **fruits** that contain a lot of vitamin C.	I bought some **fruit** at the fruit store.
Ice cream and butter are **foods** that contain cholesterol.	We don't need to go shopping today. We have a lot of **food** at home.
He wrote a **paper** about hypnosis.	I need some **paper** to write my composition.
He committed three **crimes** last year.	There is a lot of **crime** in a big city.
I have two hundred **chickens** on my farm.	We ate some **chicken** for dinner.
I don't want to bore you with all my **troubles.**	I have some **trouble** with my car.
She went to Puerto Rico three **times.**	She spent a lot of **time** on her project.
She drank three **glasses** of water.	The window is made of bulletproof **glass.**
I had a bad **experience** during my trip to Paris.	She has some **experience** with computer programming.
I don't know much about the **lives** of my grandparents.	**Life** is sometimes happy, sometimes sad.
I heard a **noise** outside my window.	Those children are making a lot of **noise.**

Use of Articles

PART 1 Use of the Indefinite Article

A. To classify a subject

Examples	Explanation
Chicago is **a** city. Illinois is **a** state. Abraham Lincoln was **an** American president.	• We use *a* before a consonant sound. • We use *an* before a vowel sound. • We can put an adjective before the noun.
Chicago and Los Angeles are cities. Lincoln and Washington were American presidents.	We do not use an article before a plural noun.

B. To make a generalization about a noun

Examples	Explanation
A dog has sharp teeth. **Dogs** have sharp teeth. **An elephant** has big ears. **Elephants** have big ears.	We use an indefinite article *(a/an)* + a singular count noun or no article with a plural noun. Both the singular and plural forms have the same meaning.
Coffee contains caffeine. **Love** makes people happy.	We do not use an article to make a generalization about a noncount noun.

C. To introduce a new noun into the conversation

Examples	Explanation
I have **a cell phone**. I have **an umbrella**.	We use the indefinite article *a/an* with singular count nouns.
I have **(some) dishes**. Do you have **(any) cups**? I don't have **(any) forks**. I have **(some) money** with me. Do you have **(any) cash** with you? I don't have **(any) time**.	We use *some* or *any* with plural nouns and noncount nouns. We use *any* in questions and negatives. *Some* and *any* can be omitted.
There's **an elevator** in the building. There isn't **any money** in my wallet.	*There* + a form of *be* can introduce an indefinite noun into a conversation.

continued

PART 2 Use of the Definite Article

A. To refer to a previously mentioned noun

Examples	Explanation
There's **a dog** in the next apartment. **The dog** barks all the time. We bought **some grapes.** We ate **the grapes** this morning.	We start by saying a *dog*. We continue by saying *the dog*. We start by saying *some grapes*. We continue by saying *the grapes*.
I need **some sugar.** I'm going to use **the sugar** to bake a cake. Did you buy **any coffee?** Yes. **The coffee** is in the cabinet.	We start by saying *some sugar*. We continue by saying *the sugar*. We start by saying *any coffee*. We continue by saying *the coffee*.

B. When the speaker and the listener have the same reference

Examples	Explanation
The number on this page is AP5.	The object is present, so the speaker and listener have the same object in mind.
The president is talking about **the** economy. Please turn off **the lights** and shut **the door** before you leave **the house**.	People who live in the same country have things in common. People who live in the same house have things in common.
The house on the corner is beautiful. I spent **the money you gave me**.	The listener knows exactly which one because the speaker defines or specifies which one.

C. When there is only one in our experience

Examples	Explanation
The sun is bigger than **the moon**. There are many problems in **the world**.	The *sun*, the *moon*, and the *world* are unique objects.
Write your name on **the top** of the page.	The page has only one top.
Alaska is **the biggest** state in the U.S.	A superlative indicates that there is only one.

D. With familiar places

Examples	Explanation
I'm going to **the store** after work. Do you need anything? **The bank** is closed now. I'll go tomorrow.	We use *the* with certain familiar places and people—*the bank, the zoo, the park, the store, the movies, the beach, the post office, the bus, the train, the doctor, the dentist*—when we refer to the one that we habitually visit or use.

Language Notes:

1. Omit *the* after a preposition with the words *church, school, work,* and *bed.*

    He's **in church**. They're **at work**.
    I'm going **to school**. I'm going **to bed**.

2. Omit *to* and *the* with *home* and *downtown.*

    I'm going **home**. Are you going **downtown** after class?

continued

E. To make a formal generalization

Examples	Explanation
The shark is the oldest and most primitive fish.	To say that something is true of all members of a group, use *the* with singular count nouns.
The computer has changed the way people deal with information.	To talk about a class of inventions, use *the.*
The ear has three parts: outer, middle, and inner.	To talk about an organ of the body in a general sense, use *the.*

Language Note:

For informal generalizations, use *a* + a singular noun or no article with a plural noun.

The computer has changed the way we deal with information. (Formal)
A computer is expensive. (Informal)
Computers are expensive. (Informal)

PART 3 Special Uses of Articles

No Article	Article
Personal names: John Kennedy	The whole family: the Kennedys
Title and name: Queen Elizabeth	Title without name: the Queen
Cities, states, countries, continents: Cleveland Ohio Mexico South America	Places that are considered a union: the United States Place names: the ________ of ________ the District of Columbia
Mountains: Mount Everest	Mountain ranges: the Rocky Mountains
Islands: Staten Island	Collectives of islands: the Hawaiian Islands
Lakes: Lake Superior	Collectives of lakes: the Great Lakes
Beaches: Palm Beach Pebble Beach	Rivers, oceans, seas: the Mississippi River the Atlantic Ocean the Dead Sea
Streets and avenues: Madison Avenue Wall Street	Well-known buildings: the Willis Tower the Empire State Building
Parks: Central Park	Zoos: the San Diego Zoo

continued

No Article	Article
Seasons: summer fall spring winter Summer is my favorite season. **Note:** After a preposition, *the* may be used. In (the) winter, my car runs badly.	Deserts: the Mojave Desert the Sahara Desert
Directions: north south east west	Sections of a piece of land: the West Side (of New York)
School subjects: history math	Unique geographical points: the North Pole the Vatican
Name + *college* or *university*: Northwestern University	The University/College of ___________ the University of Michigan
Magazines: *Time* *Sports Illustrated*	Newspapers: the *Tribune* the *Wall Street Journal*
Months and days: September Monday	Ships: the *Titanic* the *Queen Elizabeth II*
Holidays and dates: Mother's Day July 4 (month + day)	The day of month: the fifth of May the Fourth of July
Diseases: cancer AIDS polio malaria	Ailments: a cold a toothache a headache the flu
Games and sports: poker soccer	Musical instruments, after *play*: the drums the piano **Note:** Sometimes *the* is omitted. She plays (the) drums.
Languages: English	The ___________ language: the English language
Last month, year, week, etc. = the one before this one: I forgot to pay my rent last month. The teacher gave us a test last week.	The last month, the last year, the last week, etc. = the last in a series: December is the last month of the year. Vacation begins the last week in May.
In office = in an elected position: The president is in office for four years.	In the office = in a specific room: The teacher is in the office.
In back/in front: She's in back of the car.	In the back/in the front: He's in the back of the bus.

APPENDIX D

Verbs and Adjectives Followed by a Preposition

Many verbs and adjectives are followed by a preposition.		
accuse someone of	(be) familiar with	(be) prepared for/to
(be) accustomed to	(be) famous for	prevent (someone) from
adjust to	(be) fond of	prohibit (someone) from
(be) afraid of	forget about	protect (someone) from
agree with	forgive someone for	(be) proud of
(be) amazed at/by	(be) glad about	recover from
(be) angry about	(be) good at	(be) related to
(be) angry at/with	(be) grateful to someone for	rely on/upon
apologize for	(be) guilty of	(be) responsible for
approve of	(be) happy about	(be) sad about
argue about	hear about	(be) satisfied with
argue with	hear of	(be) scared of
(be) ashamed of	hope for	(be) sick of
(be) aware of	(be) incapable of	(be) sorry about
believe in	insist on/upon	(be) sorry for
blame someone for	(be) interested in	speak about
(be) bored with/by	(be) involved in	speak to/with
(be) capable of	(be) jealous of	succeed in
care about	(be) known for	(be) sure of/about
care for	(be) lazy about	(be) surprised at
compare to/with	listen to	take care of
complain about	look at	talk about
concentrate on	look for	talk to/with
(be) concerned about	look forward to	thank (someone) for
consist of	(be) mad about	(be) thankful (to someone) for
count on	(be) mad at	think about/of
deal with	(be) made from/of	(be) tired of
decide on	(be) married to	(be) upset about
depend on/upon	object to	(be) upset with
(be) different from	(be) opposed to	(be) used to
disapprove of	participate in	wait for
(be) divorced from	plan on	warn (someone) about
dream about/of	pray to	(be) worried about
(be) engaged to	pray for	worry about
(be) excited about		

Direct and Indirect Objects

The order of direct and indirect objects depends on the verb we use. It also can depend on whether we use a noun or a pronoun as the object.

Group 1	Pronouns affect word order. The preposition used is *to.*					
Patterns:	He gave a present to his wife. (DO to IO)					
	He gave his wife a present. (IO/DO)					
	He gave it to his wife. (DO to IO)					
	He gave her a present. (IO/DO)					
	He gave it to her. (DO to IO)					
Verbs:	bring	lend	pass	sell	show	teach
	give	offer	pay	send	sing	tell
	hand	owe	read	serve	take	write
Group 2	Pronouns affect word order. The preposition used is *for.*					
Patterns:	He bought a car for his daughter. (DO for IO)					
	He bought his daughter a car. (IO/DO)					
	He bought it for his daughter. (DO for IO)					
	He bought her a car. (IO/DO)					
	He bought it for her. (DO for IO)					
Verbs:	bake	buy	draw	get	make	
	build	do	find	knit	reserve	
Group 3	Pronouns don't affect word order. The preposition used is *to.*					
Patterns:	He explained the problem to his friend. (DO to IO)					
	He explained it to her. (DO to IO)					
Verbs:	admit	explain	prove	report	say	
	announce	introduce	recommend	speak		
	describe	mention	repeat	suggest		
Group 4	Pronouns don't affect word order. The preposition used is *for.*					
Patterns:	He cashed a check for his friend. (DO for IO)					
	He cashed it for her. (DO for IO)					
Verbs:	answer	change	design	open	prescribe	
	cash	close	fix	prepare	pronounce	
Group 5	Pronouns don't affect word order. No preposition is used.					
Patterns:	She asked the teacher a question. (IO/DO)					
	She asked him a question. (IO/DO)					
Verbs:	ask	charge	cost	wish	take (with time)	

APPENDIX F

Plural Forms of Nouns

Irregular Noun Plurals		
Singular	**Plural**	**Explanation**
man woman tooth foot goose	men women teeth feet geese	Vowel change (**Note:** The first vowel in *women* is pronounced /ɪ/.)
sheep fish deer	sheep fish deer	No change
child person mouse	children people (OR persons) mice	Different word form
alumnus cactus radius stimulus syllabus	alumni cacti (OR cactuses) radii stimuli syllabi (OR syllabuses)	*us* → *i*
analysis crisis hypothesis oasis parenthesis thesis	analyses crises hypotheses oases parentheses theses	*is* → *es*
appendix index	appendices (OR appendixes) indices (OR indexes)	*ix* → *ices* OR → *ixes* *ex* → *ices* OR → *exes*
bacterium curriculum datum medium memorandum criterion phenomenon	bacteria curricula data media memoranda criteria phenomena	*um* → *a* *ion* → *a* *on* → *a*
alga formula vertebra	algae formulae (OR formulas) vertebrae	*a* → *ae*

APPENDIX G

Metric Conversion Chart

Length

When You Know	Multiply by	To Find
inches (in)	2.54	centimeters (cm)
feet (ft)	30.5	centimeters (cm)
feet (ft)	0.3	meters (m)
miles (mi)	1.6	kilometers (km)
Metric:		
centimeters (cm)	0.39	inches (in)
centimeters (cm)	0.03	feet (ft)
meters (m)	3.28	feet (ft)
kilometers (km)	0.62	miles (mi)
Note: 12 inches = 1 foot 3 feet = 36 inches = 1 yard		

Weight (Mass)

When You Know	Multiply by	To Find
ounces (oz)	28.35	grams (g)
pounds (lb)	0.45	kilograms (kg)
Metric:		
grams (g)	0.04	ounces (oz)
kilograms (kg)	2.2	pounds (lb)
Note: 1 pound = 16 ounces		

continued

Volume

When You Know	Multiply by	To Find
fluid ounces (fl oz)	30.0	milliliters (mL)
pints (pt)	0.47	liters (L)
quarts (qt)	0.95	liters (L)
gallons (gal)	3.8	liters (L)
Metric:		
milliliters (mL)	0.03	fluid ounces (fl oz)
liters (L)	2.11	pints (pt)
liters (L)	1.05	quarts (qt)
liters (L)	0.26	gallons (gal)
Note: 1 pint = 2 cups 1 quart = 2 pints = 4 cups 1 gallon = 4 quarts = 8 pints = 16 cups		

Temperature

When You Know	Do this	To Find
degrees Fahrenheit (°F)	Subtract 32, then multiply by $\frac{5}{9}$	degrees Celsius (°C)
Metric:		
degrees Celsius (°C)	Multiply by $\frac{9}{5}$, then add 32	degrees Fahrenheit (°F)
Note: 32°F = 0°C 212°F = 100°C		

APPENDIX H

Irregular Verb Forms

Base Form	Past Form	Past Participle	Base Form	Past Form	Past Participle
be	was/were	been	find	found	found
bear	bore	born/borne	fit	fit	fit
beat	beat	beaten	flee	fled	fled
become	became	become	fly	flew	flown
begin	began	begun	forbid	forbade	forbidden
bend	bent	bent	forget	forgot	forgotten
bet	bet	bet	forgive	forgave	forgiven
bid	bid	bid	freeze	froze	frozen
bind	bound	bound	get	got	gotten
bite	bit	bitten	give	gave	given
bleed	bled	bled	go	went	gone
blow	blew	blown	grind	ground	ground
break	broke	broken	grow	grew	grown
breed	bred	bred	hang	hung	hung
bring	brought	brought	have	had	had
broadcast	broadcast	broadcast	hear	heard	heard
build	built	built	hide	hid	hidden
burst	burst	burst	hit	hit	hit
buy	bought	bought	hold	held	held
cast	cast	cast	hurt	hurt	hurt
catch	caught	caught	keep	kept	kept
choose	chose	chosen	know	knew	known
cling	clung	clung	lay	laid	laid
come	came	come	lead	led	led
cost	cost	cost	leave	left	left
creep	crept	crept	lend	lent	lent
cut	cut	cut	let	let	let
deal	dealt	dealt	lie	lay	lain
dig	dug	dug	light	lit/lighted	lit/lighted
dive	dove/dived	dove/dived	lose	lost	lost
do	did	done	make	made	made
draw	drew	drawn	mean	meant	meant
drink	drank	drunk	meet	met	met
drive	drove	driven	mistake	mistook	mistaken
eat	ate	eaten	overcome	overcame	overcome
fall	fell	fallen	overdo	overdid	overdone
feed	fed	fed	overtake	overtook	overtaken
feel	felt	felt	overthrow	overthrew	overthrown
fight	fought	fought	pay	paid	paid

continued

Base Form	Past Form	Past Participle
plead	pled/pleaded	pled/pleaded
prove	proved	proven/proved
put	put	put
quit	quit	quit
read	read	read
ride	rode	ridden
ring	rang	rung
rise	rose	risen
run	ran	run
say	said	said
see	saw	seen
seek	sought	sought
sell	sold	sold
send	sent	sent
set	set	set
sew	sewed	sewn/sewed
shake	shook	shaken
shed	shed	shed
shine	shone/shined	shone/shined
shoot	shot	shot
show	showed	shown/showed
shrink	shrank/shrunk	shrunk/shrunken
shut	shut	shut
sing	sang	sung
sink	sank	sunk
sit	sat	sat
sleep	slept	slept
slide	slid	slid
slit	slit	slit
speak	spoke	spoken
speed	sped	sped
spend	spent	spent
spin	spun	spun
spit	spit/spat	spit/spat
split	split	split
spread	spread	spread
spring	sprang	sprung
stand	stood	stood
steal	stole	stolen
stick	stuck	stuck

Base Form	Past Form	Past Participle
sting	stung	stung
stink	stank	stunk
strike	struck	struck/stricken
strive	strove	striven
swear	swore	sworn
sweep	swept	swept
swell	swelled	swelled/swollen
swim	swam	swum
swing	swung	swung
take	took	taken
teach	taught	taught
tear	tore	torn
tell	told	told
think	thought	thought
throw	threw	thrown
understand	understood	understood
uphold	upheld	upheld
upset	upset	upset
wake	woke	woken
wear	wore	worn
weave	wove	woven
wed	wedded/wed	wedded/wed
weep	wept	wept
win	won	won
wind	wound	wound
withdraw	withdrew	withdrawn
withhold	withheld	withheld
withstand	withstood	withstood
wring	wrung	wrung
write	wrote	written

Note:
The past and past participle of some verbs can end in *-ed* or *-t*.

burn	burned or burnt
dream	dreamed or dreamt
kneel	kneeled or knelt
learn	learned or learnt
leap	leaped or leapt
spill	spilled or spilt
spoil	spoiled or spoilt

Map of the United States of America

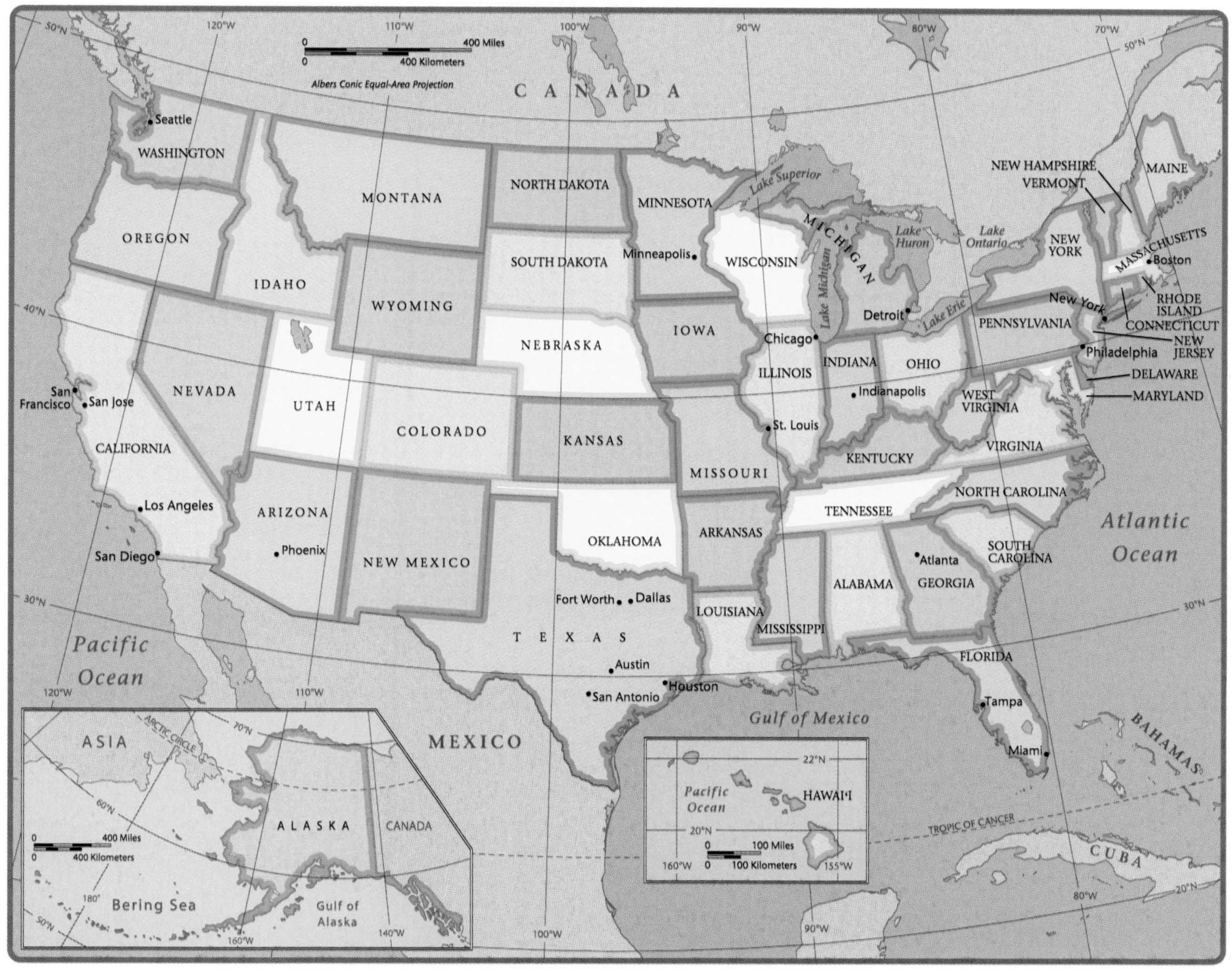

GLOSSARY

- **Adjective** An adjective gives a description of a noun.

  It's a *tall* tree. He's an *old* man. My neighbors are *nice.*

- **Adverb** An adverb describes the action of a sentence or an adjective or another adverb.

  She speaks English *fluently.* I drive *carefully.*

  She speaks English *extremely* well. She is *very* intelligent.

- **Adverb of Frequency** An adverb of frequency tells how often an action happens.

  I *never* drink coffee. They *usually* take the bus.

- **Affirmative** *Affirmative* means "yes."

  They *live* in Miami.

- **Apostrophe '** We use the apostrophe for possession and contractions.

  My *sister's* friend is beautiful. (possession)

  Today *isn't* Sunday. (contraction)

- **Article** An article comes before a noun. It tells if the noun is definite or indefinite. The definite article is *the*. The indefinite articles are *a* and *an*.

  I have *a* cat. I ate *an* apple. *The* teacher came late.

- **Auxiliary Verb** An auxiliary verb is used in forming tense, mood, or aspect of the verb that follows it. Some verbs have two parts: an auxiliary verb and a main verb.

  You *didn't* eat lunch. He *can't* study. We *will* return.

- **Base Form** The base form of the verb has no tense. It has no ending (*-s* or *-ed*): *be, go, eat, take, write.*

  I didn't *go.* We don't *know* you. He can't *drive.*

- **Capital Letter** A B C D E F G . . .

- **Clause** A clause is a group of words that has a subject and a verb. Some sentences have only one clause.

  She speaks Spanish.

  Some sentences have a **main clause** and a **dependent clause**.

MAIN CLAUSE	DEPENDENT CLAUSE **(reason clause)**
She found a good job	because she has computer skills.
MAIN CLAUSE	DEPENDENT CLAUSE **(time clause)**
She'll turn off the light	before she goes to bed.
MAIN CLAUSE	DEPENDENT CLAUSE **(*if* clause)**
I'll take you to the doctor	if you don't have your car on Saturday.

- **Colon** :
- **Comma** ,
- **Comparative** The comparative form of an adjective or adverb is used to compare two things.

  My house is *bigger* than your house.

  Her husband drives *faster* than she does.

  My children speak English *more fluently* than I do.
- **Consonant** The following letters are consonants: *b, c, d, f, g, h, j, k, l, m, n, p, q, r, s, t, v, w, x, y, z.*

  NOTE: *Y* is sometimes considered a vowel, as in the world *syllable.*
- **Contraction** A contraction is two words joined with an apostrophe.

He's my brother.	*You're* late.	They *won't* talk to me.
(*He's = he is*)	(*You're = you are*)	(*won't = will not*)
- **Count Noun** Count nouns are nouns that we can count. They have a singular and a plural form.

  1 pen–3 pens   1 table–4 tables
- **Dependent Clause** See **Clause**.
- **Direct Object** A direct object is a noun (phrase) or pronoun that receives the action of the verb.

  We saw *the movie.*   You have *a nice car.*   I love *you.*
- **Exclamation Mark** !
- **Frequency Word** Frequency words (*always, usually, generally, often, sometimes, rarely, seldom, hardly ever, never.*) tell how often an action happens.

  I *never* drink coffee.   We *always* do our homework.
- **Hyphen** -
- **Imperative** An imperative sentence gives a command or instructions. An imperative sentence omits the subject pronoun *you.*

  Come here.   *Don't be* late.   Please *help* me.
- **Infinitive** An infinitive is *to* + the base form.

  I want to *leave.*   You need *to be* here on time.
- **Linking Verb** A linking verb is a verb that links the subject to the noun, adjective, or adverb after it. Linking verbs include *be, seem, feel, smell, sound, look, appear,* and *taste.*

  She *is* a doctor.   She *looks* tired.   You *are* late.

- **Main Clause** See **Clause**.
- **Modal** The modal verbs are *can, could, shall, should, will, would, may, might,* and *must.*

  They *should* leave. I *must* go.
- **Negative** *Negative* means "no."
- **Nonaction Verb** A nonaction verb has no action. We do not use a continuous tense (*be* + verb *-ing*) with a nonaction verb. The nonaction verbs are: *believe, cost, care, have, hear, know, like, love, matter, mean, need, own, prefer, remember, see, seem, think, understand, want,* and sense-perception verbs.

  She *has* a laptop. We *love* our mother. You *look* great.
- **Noncount Noun** A noncount noun is a noun that we don't count. It has no plural form.

  She drank some *water.* He prepared some *rice.*

  Do you need any *money*? We had a lot of *homework.*
- **Noun** A noun is a person, a place, or a thing. Nouns can be either count or noncount.

  My *brother* lives in California. My *sisters* live in New York.

  I get *advice* from them. I drink *coffee* every day.
- **Noun Modifier** A noun modifier makes a noun more specific.

  fire department *Independence* Day *can* opener
- **Noun Phrase** A noun phrase is a group of words that form the subject or object of the sentence.

  A very nice woman helped me. I bought *a big box of cereal.*
- **Object** The object of the sentence follows the verb. It receives the action of the verb.

  He bought *a car.* I saw *a movie.* I met *your brother.*
- **Object Pronoun** We use object pronouns (*me, you, him, her, it, us, them*) after the verb or preposition.

  He likes *her.* I saw the movie. Let's talk about *it.*
- **Parentheses** ( )
- **Paragraph** A paragraph is a group of sentences about one topic.
- **Past Participle** The past participle of a verb is the third form of the verb.

  You have *written* a good essay. I was *told* about the concert.
- **Period** .
- **Phrasal Modal** Phrasal modals, such as *ought to, be able to,* are made up of two or more words.

  You *ought to* study more. We *have to* take a test.
- **Phrase** A group of words that go together.

  Last month my sister came to visit. There is a strange car *in front of my house.*
- **Plural** *Plural* means "more than one." A plural noun usually ends with *-s.*

  She has beautiful *eyes.* My *feet* are big.

- **Possessive Form** Possessive forms show ownership or relationship.

  Mary's coat is in the closet. *My* brother lives in Miami.

- **Preposition** A preposition is a short connecting word. Some common prepositions include *about, above, across, after, around, as, at, away, back, before, behind, below, by, down, for, from, in, into, like, of, off, on, out, over, to, under, up,* and *with.*

  The book is *on* the table. She studies *with* her friends.

- **Present Participle** The present participle of a verb is the base form + *-ing.*

  She is *sleeping.* They were *laughing.*

- **Pronoun** A pronoun takes the place of a noun.

  I have a new car. I bought *it* last week.

  John likes Mary, but *she* doesn't like *him.*

- **Punctuation** The use of specific marks, such as commas and periods, to make ideas within writing clear.

- **Question Mark** ?

- **Quotation Marks** " "

- **Regular Verb** A regular verb forms its past tense with *-ed.*

  He *worked* yesterday. I *laughed* at the joke.

- ***-s* Form** A present tense verb that ends in *-s* or *-es.*

  He *lives* in New York. She *watches* TV a lot.

- **Sense-Perception Verb** A sense-perception verb has no action. It describes a sense. The sense-perception verbs are: *look, feel, taste, sound,* and *smell.*

  She *feels* fine. The coffee *smells* fresh. The milk *tastes* sour.

- **Sentence** A sentence is a group of words that contains a subject and a verb and gives a complete thought.

  SENTENCE: She came home.

  NOT A SENTENCE: When she came home

- **Singular** *Singular* means "one."

  She ate a *sandwich.* I have one *television.*

- **Subject** The subject of the sentence tells who or what the sentence is about.

  My sister got married last April. *The wedding* was beautiful.

- **Subject Pronoun** We use a subject pronoun (*I, you, he, she, it, we, you, they*) before a verb.

  They speak Japanese. *We* speak Spanish.

- **Superlative** The superlative form of an adjective or adverb shows the number one item in a group of three or more.

  January is the *coldest* month of the year.

  My brother speaks English the *best* in my family.

- **Syllable** A syllable is a part of a word. Each syllable has only one vowel sound. (Some words have only one syllable.)

  change (one syllable) after (af·ter = two syllables)

  look (one syllable) responsible (re·spon·si·ble = four syllables)

- **Tag Question** A tag question is a short question at the end of a sentence. It is used in conversation.

  You speak Spanish, *don't you*? He's not happy, *is he*?

- **Tense** Tense shows when the action of the sentence happened. Verbs have different tenses.

  SIMPLE PRESENT: She usually *works* hard.

  PRESENT CONTINUOUS: She *is working* now.

  SIMPLE PAST: She *worked* yesterday.

  FUTURE: She *will work* tomorrow.

- **Verb** A verb is the action of the sentence.

  He *runs* fast. I *speak* English.

- **Vowel** The following letters are vowels: *a, e, i, o, u.*

  NOTE: *Y* is sometimes considered a vowel, as in the world *syllable.*

INDEX

Note: All page references in blue are in Split Edition B.

O

P

Q

Y